Your Spiritual Lineage: Researching the Genealogy of Your Soul

Your Spiritual Lineage: Researching the Genealogy of Your Soul

Pioneering a New Understanding of the Origins of Personality Development

William E. Bray

In Association with Bilbo Books

iUniverse, Inc.

New York Lincoln Shanghai

Your Spiritual Lineage: Researching the Genealogy of Your Soul
Pioneering a New Understanding of the Origins of Personality Development

Copyright © 2006 by William E. Bray

iUniverse books may be ordered through booksellers or by contacting:

iUniverse
2021 Pine Lake Road, Suite 100
Lincoln, NE 68512
www.iuniverse.com
1-800-Authors (1-800-288-4677)

ISBN-13: 978-0-595-39516-3 (pbk)
ISBN-13: 978-0-595-83915-5 (ebk)
ISBN-10: 0-595-39516-3 (pbk)
ISBN-10: 0-595-83915-0 (ebk)

Printed in the United States of America

Contents

Acknowledgments

Many people have been supportive of my efforts for 20 years to provide educational and enriching courses for visual and performing arts students, for at-risk inner city students, and for students who were part of the public school system's program for emotionally and behaviorally disabled students. Without the help of three people I could not have accomplished that nor been able to proceed with this book. I would like to acknowledge their incredible support and express my deepest appreciation for their help. They are Harold M. Shapiro, Dr. Philip Bates Bailey and James R. (Rusty) Barber. Others who have been very supportive during this period are my father J. Wellborn Bray, Sr., Dr. Patrick G. Bray, Dr. Bette R. Bonder, Barbara Day Smith, Lourinda Bray, Dr. Ed Miron and Tom Lambert, Jr. Many others provided contributions and volunteer efforts toward these goals, and I would like to express my appreciation to them.

In the late 1990's, it was Dr. Candice Shoemaker, then head of the horticulture department at Berry College, who said, "A friend from Charleston recommended I read *Many Lives, Many Masters* by Dr. Brian Weiss. I think you would like it. I think you should read it." I am grateful to her for this recommendation. It started me on my "reading journey" which resulted in this book.

I would also like to acknowledge those friends who, over the years, have patiently listened, expressed their input and encouragement, and been supportive in my ongoing research culminating in this book. They are Tory Tepp, Ann Byrd, Jason Graham, Bowen Craig, Penny Carpenter, Allan Moye, Marshall Gorges, The Reverend Frederick J.

Hanna, Jim Moon, John Chapman, Mary and Bob James, Deborah Lewis, Mike Moran, Curt Arey, Dean and Judson Moss, Myra Shapiro, Dr. Richard Brouillard, Kyle Caswell, Alan Stone, Eric Phelps, and Alan Rieger. Dr. Jim Tucker on the faculty at the University of Virginia, and The Reverend Dr. Larry J. Kreitzer, tutor of New Testament at Regent's Park College, Oxford University were also helpful. Especially supportive was The Reverend Jane A. Shaw, then on the faculty of Regent's Park College at Oxford and on the staff of St. Mary the Virgin Church, and now Chaplain of New College, who was very encouraging and stressed the importance more than once of my publishing this book.

Finally, I would like to express my appreciation to members of Jennifer French Echols' writers group in Atlanta, and to Bill York of the Georgia Writers Association and Katie Egan at iUniverse for the technical support.

Preface

The naysayers, the skeptics, and those who have made science their religion and belief in the myth of "proof" their means of denying mystery and removing a sense of wonder from their lives, may have trouble with this book. It is not a typical New Age nor metaphysical book, rather I start with Socrates and Plato, who accepted belief in and acceptance of past and future lives as normal. It is unfortunate that academics have to rely on pedantic baby steps in the advancement of knowledge, afraid to venture too far from what others have accomplished before them. A mountain of footnotes suggest a mental game of building blocks of others' findings, rather than an adventure in imagination and intuition. If we do have within each of our subconscious recollections and repressed memories of experience and knowledge gained during 80 or more previous lifetimes stretching back through centuries and even millennia, then we have a wealth of knowledge at our disposals. Such stores of knowledge are within each of us, if we only knew how to recall or access them. In Plato's Dialogue *Phaedo* the argument that Socrates often put forward is repeated—that learning is recollection. This innate knowledge, he contends, must have been learned in some previous time somewhere before appearing in this human frame, an argument proving, he contends, that the soul seems to be immortal. Socrates' argument stresses the importance of remembering to learning and its essential function in gaining knowledge.

This remembering is the key function, though often unrealized, in the best of artists. In the case with Virgil, he is simply remembering his earlier past life and adventures as Alcibiades, and later Alexander the

Great, naming him Aeneas in his literary retelling of them in the Aeneid. This book is intended to help you explore how to open the magical door to your memories from past lives. It will also illuminate your daily activities, showing how your every thought, word and deed, including every decision you make, has its origins before you were born.

For more than five years I served as a psychology professor at two colleges and an instructor in psychology and humanities at a third. The courses I taught included General Psychology, Child Psychology, Adolescent Psychology, and Psychology of Religion. In addition, I had studied psychology as part of my Master of Divinity degree at Yale and in post graduate study at Oxford, where Ian Ramsey at Oriel College was my tutor (the Ian Ramsey Centre of Religion and Science studies is named for him). In virtually all of these courses and educational experiences the traditional understanding of the beginning of personality starts at birth. Freud even divides the first five years of life into three phases, showing how each dramatically affects personality development.

Years later, when I read *Many Lives, Many Masters,* a case study of one of his patients by Dr. Brian Weiss, a psychiatrist in Miami, I was amazed. His patient, under hypnosis, had gone back beyond her earliest recollections of childhood to past lives to "remember" the source of her psychological problems. Her phobias resulted from traumatic death experiences she was remembering subconsciously from previous lifetimes. Helping her remember these traumas led to a dramatically improved condition for her. Dr. Weiss then pursued other patients with cases of phobias, finding answers and similar relief from their symptoms no one had discovered before. Consequently, he has pioneered the field of "regression therapy."

There is no doubting Dr. Weiss' scientific credentials—graduating from Columbia Phi Beta Kappa, magna cum laude, then Yale University's School of Medicine for his M. D., internship at New York University-Bellevue Medical Center and back to Yale for his residency in psychiatry. Reading *Many Lives, Many Masters* started me on a virtual "reading journey" of more than 45 subsequent books in a quest for a better understanding of this phenomenon.

I recognized Dr. Brian Weiss' work as an opening to a larger past life knowledge that could explain more than just the cause of phobias, but to an understanding of virtually the whole development of personality. If we have repressed memories in our unconscious of 86 lifetimes (the number of past lives his patient could remember) or more, then those repressed memories are impacting on our thoughts, feelings, emotions, and choices we make 24 hours a day. Not only are these memories causing neuroses, they are leading us in choices of professions and educational preparations for them, locations where we choose to live, our choices of travel for pleasure, and more. Suddenly, we can understand child prodigies—they are remembering at an early age skills and knowledge they gained in a past life or several past lives.

Metaphysical writers suggest even more intriguing notions—that we are conscious "in between" lifetimes, and that we return to each new lifetime in a "soul group." They suggest that we reconnoiter with that soul group between lives and map out our individual and group missions for the next one. Our spirit entities (consisting of our "personalities") may be hurtling down through time with predetermined missions. We may be destined to meet and join others in our "soul group" in pursuit of that mission. It may be an ongoing mission from one lifetime to the next being refined and redefined in and for each new generation.

Psychologist Carl Jung developed theories of archetypes and the collective unconscious exploring some of these possibilities. If our bodies have minds that are capable of storing emotional fragments of memories of past lives going back hundreds and thousands of years, then we have, stored in our unconscious, an educational storehouse of history that can make A&E's Biography and the History Channel look like kindergarten. Such may have been the knowledge of Socrates when he proposed that recollection is at the core of learning. If this is the case, then each of us was an eyewitness to history and a sculptor in its making.

It is my hope that *Your Spiritual Lineage* will be viewed as a door opener to a new field in psychology, a new study of personality development: the study of **pre-childhood psychology**. Many children still have past life memories when they are born and refer to their previous life-time, describing it as "when I was big." Dr. Jim Tucker at the University of Virginia faculty travels around the world interviewing some of these children and has written a book entitled *Life Before Life*. A teacher in a private school in Atlanta once told me that her young pre-school daughter spoke frequently of "when she was big. I encourage her to speak freely," she said, "because I know that when she gets to school, teachers and students will laugh at her, and she will no longer be able to remember." Past life memories may be the subject of dreams or the reason people choose to write biographies (to set the record straight of accounts of their past lives) or advance scientific theories they may have begun developing before but died before their work was completed or their mission accomplished.

If we are drawn to places we've lived, studied or traveled to before, then we are "walking on our own faded footprints without knowing it." When I was in Prague, studying at Charles University in 2000, after several days I was brave enough to share these ideas with my newly assigned roommate. I further tested his intellectual depth, capacities and resilience by saying I thought I had been Guillaume Apollinaire in my most recent previous lifetime. Several days later he came running into the room, saying that he had been assigned Prague's Café Slavia as the topic for a term paper and learned that Apollinaire had eaten there regularly. I was astounded, since I had not even known Apollinaire had ever been to Prague, yet now I had been walking over his faded foot-prints—even eating at his favorite restaurant without knowing that he had eaten there regularly.

Dr. Brian Weiss, with his impeccable scientific credentials has already opened the door to past life study. I propose we take the study of psychology to worlds where Freud and Adler had not thought to trod by establishing a new field in the study of personality development, that of **pre-childhood psychology**—not just as therapy for phobic or other neurotic symptoms, but for a broader understanding of who we are and what life is about—our place in time and the universe.

In *Your Spiritual Lineage: Researching the Genealogy of Your Soul* I use genealogical research techniques I've learned and used as a professional genealogist. Using the New Age concept of "soul group" as a virtual "spirit family", in my research I search for the same key relationships like in genealogy one would search for a family member. I am suggesting we use these historical research techniques to explore the clues, which are around us all the time, to past life memories. The book also explores two spiritual lineages in history as examples of how this research can be done. Each chapter concludes with a Lessons Learned section as the author and reader move toward increased understanding and use of these historical research techniques.

It is my hope that this will not only lead to a new approach to psychology, but provide a new way of looking at history. Hopefully, it will lead to a better understanding of history, if we are able to recognize the reappearance of dynamic personalities and their missions in successive lifetimes, as they (all of us) come hurtling down through time.

Introduction

It was my day off as director of an arts center on the Delaware Coast, and I had driven across the flatlands of the Delmarva Pennisular to have dinner at an inn in Oxford, Maryland. The tiny hamlet of Oxford had a main street with stores on one side and a park leading down to the Chesapeake Bay on the other. After dinner I sat on a park bench facing the bay watching the sun disappearing on the other shore and the mellowing of the day into dusk. I began to think about my life and where I was going. I had been in the northeast for 15 years. What were things like in my native Georgia? The years of the Civil Rights Movement—freedom rides and lunch counter sit-ins—had raged across the South. My family and I had become alienated over this issue and others. There would need to be reconciling, fence mending, dealing with people who had not been away from Georgia as I had. I would be leaving friends with whom I could carry on all kinds of conversations.

I had decided my senior year at the University of Georgia what to do with my life. I would embark on an educational odyssey starting at Yale Divinity School, and including additional degrees and studies, working in cultural centers of the world, and traveling as much as possible—to "deprovincialize myself and absorb culture like a sponge," in what I called Phase I of my life. The thought of returning to Georgia to begin Phase II had not crossed my mind in years. I had forgotten about it.

As darkness settled, and as I began driving my car eastward toward Rehoboth Beach, Delaware, back toward the Atlantic Ocean, passing through the cool summer night with my windows down, smelling the clear, crisp air of the flat sandy land of the Delmarva Pennisula, I started to think. Slowly, as though I were reasoning with myself, I began to realize, "I have been here for 15 years. I have achieved everything I set out to do. I came here TO GO BACK. The purpose of my being here is to go back." But I did not want to go back. I wanted to stay with my friends I had made over 15 years and to still be able to go to plays and museums in New York any weekend I wanted to.

And then as my body began to stiffen at the thought of returning and to rebel at the thought, I began to ask a further question, "What is life all about? Are we here to FEED THE SENSES, OR to help other people, and TRY TO MAKE THIS A BETTER WORLD?" Then, I began to become angry, because I knew what the answer to that question was for me. For me there was not even any consideration; it was clear. I was here to do what I could to try to make this a better world. By this time, I had driven up onto the bridge over the Choptank River in Denton, Maryland. At this moment, I knew for the first time since I had been away, it was time to go back! But I did not want to go back!!! It had been the farthermost thought from my mind that morning as I had driven out of Rehoboth Beach on my day off. And here, in a matter of hours, my life had been completely turned around.

My body weakened, as I drove down off that bridge over the Choptank River. Driving up a block toward the courthouse square, I was having trouble moving my legs in order to push the accelerator. I struggled to get my foot onto the brake to slow the car down, and then I pulled into a parking place in front of the courthouse. I was so dazed by the enormity of what I was now facing that I struggled to get out of the car. Once I got out and stood up alongside the car, I fell. Only the side of the car kept me from hitting the ground.

I DID NOT WANT TO GO BACK!

I returned to Rehoboth Beach and phoned my friends in Baltimore, and they all thought I had lost my mind. "You've had too much sun at the beach. Come back to Baltimore."

But two months later, I began packing. I returned to live at an historic farm and gardens in northwest Georgia, which had been in my family for generations. Phase II of my life, I had decided, would be to use the education I had acquired in the Northeast and to use this historic place, as an instrument, in my goal of doing what I could to make this a better world for the next generation. That had been 20 years before. I returned to Georgia and established myself in the arts—the logical use of the farm's old historic garden, which included a 200 year old house and 25 acres of daffodils, which bloomed every spring. I formed a non-profit organization, where we used the farm in the 1980's to train high school students gifted in the arts, and in the 1990's, students who were at-risk and who were emotionally and behaviorally disabled, using the arts and hikes on the farm to give focus and meaning to their lives.

After 15 years conducting these programs, one evening, I drove down to Rome, a city nearby in northwest Georgia, to have dinner with a friend who was on the faculty of one of the colleges there. She told me about watching one of the interview programs on television. The guests had been two children who could speak foreign and ancient languages without ever having been exposed to them. As a scientist, she was fascinated and wondered how this could happen. A friend of hers had recommended a book, *Many Lives, Many Masters* by Dr. Brian Weiss. "You should get it," she said, "I think you would really like it."

The next time I was in Atlanta, I stopped by my favorite bookstore. I asked at the counter where the book was located, surprised that I had remembered the author and the title so easily without having written them down. "Right over there," I was told by one of the helpers. I walked over to where he had pointed, saw the book, and immediately picked it up. As I was thumbing through it, I looked up at the sign over the section of books. In big, bold letters it read: **New Age.** I nervously looked around to see if anybody was looking. I had always made fun of friends who had read any of this kind of literature, and I had thought it was "far out." But, then I thought, "Wait a minute. I am an adult. I can handle this." And I stopped worrying about what anybody thought who might see me reading a NEW AGE book.

What I soon realized was that New Age is not New Age at all, but this genre of literature describes some of the oldest concepts and writings in philosophy. So, in a way, "New Age" is just "Old Age" rediscovered. It is a rediscovery of old and eternal truths. Before I finished reading Dr. Brian Weiss' *Many Lives, Many Masters*, I knew what I was going to read next, and while I was reading Dr. Weiss' second book, I knew what I was going to read after that. Twenty books later, as I was reading each book, knowing what I was to read next, I was amazed. "What is this?" I asked. "What is going on? What do I have here? This is a phenomenon that I don't understand. Never in college, never at any time in my life, have I read like this." Soon, I was making a list, and as I finished each book, I would add it to the list with notes beside the most recent two: "currently reading" and "to be read next." I told friends as I would send them updated copies of the list I had read, "I don't know what's going on or what this is, but I could teach it."

And then, one day I looked at the list and knew what it was. Two days later a friend came to the farm, and I showed her the list of books I had read on this "reading journey." "You know what you should do?" my friend asked. "You should write a book."

"I know," I said. What I had realized I had in my hands was a BIBLIOGRAPHY. What I knew I should do was write a book. What you are holding in your hands is that book.

In the following pages you will see not only a reading journey unfold, but a journey that leads into past lives. Soon, I discovered that one of my own former students had been the French poet Arthur Rimbaud in a past life. Before that he had been Alexander the Great, and other leaders and writers of the past. This is not fiction. It is the true story of my research and subsequent discoveries and findings. Only the names of some contemporary persons may have been changed to provide them anonymity and to protect their privacy.

My former student, whom I concluded was the French poet Arthur Rimbaud, has exhibited behavior we might, under ordinary circumstances, consider unusual, but in light of discovering his SPIRITUAL LINEAGE understandable. I realized that he was walking on his own faded footprints—repeating travels, personality traits, leadership qualities that had in earlier lifetimes helped shape our world. Not only he, but all of us do this.

We are living in a world in which we are seeing without SEEING. It is an age of practicality. Coincidences—emphasized by authors Brian Weiss and James Redfield—are not only wake up calls from a spiritual dimension we cannot see, which surrounds us, but coincidences carry messages within themselves, if we but train ourselves to recognize them. Through these pages, I would like to share the journey I have made over the past few years. That journey is still is progress, as I discover new lifetimes on the spiritual lineage chart.

In reading this account, be thinking of your own clues, your own path. Examine your own life purpose—your mission. Think not in terms of doing the same thing all of your life, but think of your life as phases of one continuing mission, or a succession of missions. The different phases of your life may reflect influences of different past times, or a succession of missions that you are accomplishing. Many of the writers in my reading journey believe that each of us is a member of a soul group consisting of seven to 25 people that keeps returning together. We may be the main player in the group mission in one lifetime, but on the periphery of the group in the next. We may have a life that is so intense in one generation, we need a rest period in the next. Remember that everyone cannot be an Alexander the Great in each lifetime.

My role in this lifetime, as a teacher, has been to be a cheerleader, a supporter for students in the arts. Often this includes urging them to surge forward even though there may be opposition in what they want to do with their lives from parents, friends, or the society as a whole, which now seems to be stressing economic success above all other forms of accomplishments. In exasperation once with a very talented student, I exclaimed, "What? Are you going to just sit out this lifetime? Are you going to just pass in this lifetime?" Gradually, his talents, as an artist, have been put on a shelf, as he is being increasingly seduced by the material rewards of economic success.

So, the reader should not think that he or she has no place to begin, because he or she does not now occupy some post on the pinnacle of public recognition. Remember that Vincent Van Gogh was considered a failure as a painter to his contemporaries during his lifetime. If we could but remember what we have learned in our past lifetimes, how profound would be our abilities to survive and excel. It is my hope and goal that this book will help you realize that end. Use my journey as a roadmap and guide—a "how-to manual." In your hand you hold the record of my spiritual journey, but you have a journey to make too. Let this be *your* beginning.

1

your poor Arthur Rimbaud

In 1997 I was visiting a friend in Rehoboth Beach, Delaware, when she suggested we go to Ocean City, Maryland to see a new movie made on the familiar story line of *The Secret Garden*. It was made by a filmmaker from Poland, who then lived in Paris, Agnieska Holland. I was most impressed with the film. It had a clear story line. It was well cast. Of previous productions of the story, I felt it was clearly the best. So impressed was I with it, that I made a point to see her earlier films, and became enthusiastic about her work—looking for her next movie after *The Secret Garden*.

A year later while scanning the new movies available at a local video store, I saw, to my surprise, a new film out on video made by Agnieska Holland. It was entitled *Total Eclipse,* a film about the French poet Arthur Rimbaud. Rimbaud was played by the actor Leonardo DiCaprio, who was virtually the same age while making the movie that Rimbaud was in that part of his life the movie depicted.

I knew little about Rimbaud, except that he was a French poet. I had never read any of his work, nor had I studied him or his poetry in any class I had taken. So, my knowledge of Rimbaud was like a blank book, waiting for me to learn from this film. I was very moved by the film. As I watched it, I was extremely impressed by the realistic way in which it portrayed the painful difficulty which people have in trying to relate to one another. The film also gave examples of the best depictions I had ever seen in a motion picture of premonition and apparition.

The following day, I was driving to nearby Rome, Georgia, and when I stopped for a traffic light, I found myself crying. It was happening before I realized it. I had been extremely affected by the movie *Total Eclipse*, which I had seen the day before, but I had never been moved like this by any film I had ever seen. I had been left subconsciously in great pain, though I didn't fully understand why.

I proceeded to the restaurant where I was headed for lunch, and, after ordering my lunch, and while eating, I found myself crying again. This was somewhat embarrassing, since I was surrounded by other people, and I tried to subtly wipe away the tears that were streaming down my face. "What was going on?" I asked myself. I had never had a reaction like this to a movie—to anything! What was there about this poet—his life, his story—which had moved me this deeply? Initially, I had thought the story of his life affected me because of difficulties I had seen during my lifetime of people around me trying to get along. But now, I realized it was something more…something much deeper, much more profound. The answer must rest in Rimbaud himself, the subject of the film. I drove straight to the book store from having lunch and bought *Arthur Rimbaud: Complete Works*. I drove home and began reading the book that afternoon. Somewhere in the life story of Arthur Rimbaud something had touched a nerve deep inside me. I was searching for what that was.

As I read I was also educating myself on Rimbaud, poetry and French poetry. I was later to learn that in Rimbaud, his life and poetry, the entire Surrealist Movement in Art had its foundations. Before I read the book of Rimbaud's poetry that day, I had read about his life in the Encyclopedia Britannica, and even that brief description of his life led me to tears. I was astonished that a single life—one whose creative outburst would have such a short span, ceasing by age 19 when he stropped writing poetry—could be that dramatic and powerful. Later that night, as I was reading one of Rimbaud's poems, my heart seemed to stop. I had read a line in one of his poems, which recently had come straight out of the mouth of one of my former students and friends.

Alex at 14 had been the youngest student in our program in 1984. He was awed by the knowledge of the older art students, but by the end of the three week program, he had gained confidence. In a televised interview about the program, his enthusiasm, his command of language and his ability to express himself was without doubt the best of any student I had ever had. After the program that summer his family moved several times over the next few years, but he made a point to keep in touch. Whether his family was in Wisconsin, Iowa or Florida, he phoned or came by at least twice a year. When he decided to choose an art school for his undergraduate education, he phoned me from Iowa. I recommended an art school in New York. He applied, was accepted and offered a scholarship. The spring after he had been accepted, he came by the farm to see me. As we sat on the porch looking out over the glen and springs with leaves of trees beginning to bud and flowers blooming, he seemed to vibrate, if not glow, when he told me how he felt. "I am so excited! I feel as though fire is flowing through my veins!"

Now, seven years later, I was reading his same words and others that Alex had spoken to me that afternoon, and now I was realizing they had been written in a poem by Arthur Rimbaud more than a century before. When I read Rimbaud's poem "IT WAS SPRINGTIME," I could hear the voice of my friend and former student Alex saying them to me that day on the porch as he eagerly anticipated going to school in New York. Neither he nor I realized he was repeating word for word, what Rimbaud had written on November 6, 1868, at the age of 14. Rimbaud had written them in Latin "VER ERAT" and with it he won the First Prize in Latin Composition.

Not all at once, but gradually, the thought came to me. "Could it be possible that my friend and former student Alex, could be a reincarnation of the famous French poet Arthur Rimbaud?"

I had read *Many Lives, Many Masters* by Brian Weiss, the Miami psychiatrist who had founded the method of regression therapy based upon the acceptance of past lives—that one's spirit is eternal, and that it comes back over and over again each time in a new body—to grow in knowledge and love. I had also read the works of James Redfield, whose pioneering book *The Celestine Prophecy* had presented current new age tenets in a fictional adventure parable. Among these is the concept of a soul group—that our spirits are part of a "soul group" of seven to twenty-five spirits, who not only have individual missions but group missions as well in each lifetime. I had been a passionate genealogist and had done professional genealogical research. This had taken me to the New York Public Library, Library of Congress, Georgia State Archives, Chattanooga Public Library, but my favorite place was the Alderman Library at the University of Virginia in Charlottesville. There at the end of a tiring day in the stacks I could retire to Thomas Jefferson's The Lawn and "observe dusk." I was convinced that Charlottesville is an example of one of James Redfield's "sacred places."

Historical research was as natural as breathing for me, so almost instinctively I thought: "If Alex is a reincarnation of Arthur Rimbaud, and I have had such a pivotal role in Alex's life, then could I not have been someone in a comparable position in the life of Arthur Rimbaud?" If I could find such a person in Rimbaud's life, then it would give more credence to this wild notion that was now developing in my mind.

Over years of genealogical research I had developed a speed method of researching "family trees." I loved genealogical research. It was like a detective story, a treasure hunt and an intellectual game all in one. It was an adventure to me—exciting, fun—better than bridge, monopoly or golf. Genealogy had the added benefit of increasing our knowledge and dealing with the most important questions a person can ask: "Who am I?" Now, I was using the same techniques, passion and enthusiasm to ask an even more important question: "Who was I in previous lifetimes, and what is the mission or purpose of my eternal spirit in past, present and future lifetimes?" It occurred to me that I could research a person's spiritual lineage by using the relationships of his "soul group" as clues, the same way one would look at one's "family" members in genealogical research. If I was on the right track, then I should be able to find a teacher in Rimbaud's life, who "discovered" his talents, and relentlessly supported his interest in his art (in Rimbaud's case, poetry), as I had done with Alex in this lifetime.

This involved more than simply reading a book of his poetry, and so I was off to the library in Rome looking for a person in Rimbaud's life, whom I wasn't sure existed. As I opened books of Rimbaud's biography, I read that he was born in Charleville, France in 1854 and had died in Marseille in 1891. Not only did I find that there was a teacher and mentor in Rimbaud's life, comparable to me, who had discovered his talents and opened his library to him as I had done for Alex, but I found myself reading letters Rimbaud had written to him. His first teacher who "discovered" his talents was Georges Izambard.

Izambard, his teacher, had met Rimbaud when he was 14, the same age Alex was when I had met him. Georges Izambard had not only listened to him discuss his ideas, and opened his library to him, but one time had taken him to live with his aunts—encouraging him in every way he could as I had done in trying to help Alex. And then I read a letter Rimbaud had written to Georges Izambard when he was 15. He had gotten arrested for getting off a train and not having enough money for his ticket. He pleaded with Izambard saying he had always been like a brother, saying he loved him like a brother and would love him like a father, if he would just help him. He signed the letter your poor Arthur Rimbaud. It was sent from prison in Mazas.

By the time I finished reading the letter tears were streaming down my face and onto the page. This was not an impersonal reaction to these words. Not only were tears streaming down my face, but shivers were going up and down my spine. I realized that this was not the first time I had read this letter. I had read it before…from the depths of my soul…I REMEMBERED! I realized I would have read it before, in Rimbaud's own handwriting, when I would have lived in Charleville, France in 1869. I had found the duplicated relationship I had sought. I had no other explanations for the powerful depth of feeling that moved my soul at these words and the actions of a 15–year-old poet who had lived a century before in France, unless I had been Georges Izambard, Rimbaud's teacher in that lifetime.

I began almost instinctively and without thought to put the mechanics of my genealogical research techniques to work. In area libraries I found every book I could find on the life of Arthur Rimbaud and studied his poetry and personality traits. Part of my genealogical research technique involved developing a hypothetical scenario as soon as possible of the life and movements of the person you were studying, and see if you can find historical facts to support the accuracy of your projected scenario. You affirm or reject your scenario as you progress in your research depending on what you find or do not find. This method gives excitement, drama and fun to your research. In short, you turn it into a game.

Now I had developed a scenario. If Alex were a reincarnation of Arthur Rimbaud, I was sure that certain life patterns would be repeated and certain tastes or "likes" or "dislikes" that Alex had would be the result of unconscious "memory." He would be remembering them on a subconscious level and be familiar with them without knowing it consciously. So my genealogical method "detective story research" would involve looking at Alex's personality traits, comparing his ideas, his likes and dislikes, to that of the young French poet when he was in his teens, the period in his life when Rimbaud wrote all of his poetry. By this time Alex was 21 and an art student living in New York.

The next time I was in New York, Alex's art school was having a student exhibition. I remember the excitement of walking into the large expansive gallery filled with scores of paintings of emerging artists from all over the United States at this, one of the best art schools in the country. When I walked in even without surveying the walls of paintings my eyes were drawn straight across the gallery to several paintings that seemed to vibrate. I knew they belonged to Alex. Their colors and forms were human, sexual, vibrant, almost violent with energy. They were new, different. They were different from all the other paintings by the other students. When I later analyzed it, I realized the other students had painted exactly the kind of work you would expect from first year art school students—as though they were completing an assignment. But Alex's paintings looked and felt like they were on fire.

When Alex and I had time to sit down at a coffee shop near Washington Square, he was filled with enthusiasm about his interests in the occult, magic, Eastern mysticism and philosophy. His art dramatically reflected this interest. Preparing for this meeting, I had just read of how Rimbaud had ceased to study literature, but he had studied occult philosophy, magic and the Cabala. He had devoured these books as avidly as he had his previous studies. For nearly an hour I listened to hair raising descriptions of the things in which he was now absorbed. His interest in them were all repeating, to the year, the changing patterns of Rimbaud's interests, confirming my hypothetical scenario. I continued to test my hypothesis by cautiously asking, "Have you heard of or ever studied Arthur Rimbaud?" He looked at me surprised and said, "Why, yes. I organized a poetry reading among fellow students as soon as I got to New York, and I opened our first session by reading from my favorite of Rimbaud's poems, "The Drunken Boat." He had recited it from memory, and then he recited it from memory for me. As we sat huddled over our coffees, I could feel the hairs on my arms standing up, as he spoke.

I continued to study everything I could about Rimbaud, trying to understand the depth of my feelings (especially if I were a reincarnation of Georges Izambard). This took me to area libraries, the internet, to the Emory University library and the Johns Hopkins University library (which had 179 books on Arthur Rimbaud). I could not believe that so much energy existed in such a small boy, and that such a volume of creative energy had exploded in him in such a short time. He seemed to have amplified a hundredfold the passion, the need to be loved and to love, the hurt and the pain, and the openness that many of us more ordinary persons have. It is not surprising that artists and sensitive persons of all persuasions have been drawn to him.

I marveled as I read Rimbaud's poetry and realized why it changed the world of poetry. He speaks of dying of love and seems to carry on a conversation with a flower and a bird above. His poems from the age of ten describe spring and nature with a clarity and sensitivity unmatched in poetry. Then, in one of his poems, he seems to describe the heavens as virtually opening with the declaration that he is to be a poet.

Georges Izambard was drawn to this bright young sensitve 14 year old student, being a perfect mentor and friend. But when Rimbaud joined the militia, he went one evening to the barracks with other soldiers, and being young and frail, he was violated by the soldiers. This experience devastated him. He sought to put his feelings in a poem which he sent to Izambard with a letter. The letter was sent on May 13, 1871.

Then, in this letter to Izambard, Rimbaud implored him not to be the academic and underline with a pencil. He attached his horrific poem about his ordeal in the barracks. As I read the ending of the poem, I felt the pain, again, this time, from understanding. The poem was entitled THE STOLEN HEART.

Izambard read the poem, but never suspected that it was based on an actual event. Arthur expected his teacher to be sensitive enough and alert enough to see that it was based on the actual experience that had happened to him without his being told, but Izambard began to read it as though it were a classroom exercise. Arthur was so hurt that his dear and close friend had failed to understand his deepest wound that he terminated his relationship with him. It occurred to me that my own extreme reaction to anything I was reading and seeing about Arthur Rimbaud would be the outpouring of my own hurt and disappointment in myself that I (as Georges Izambard) had failed a student and friend in an hour of deepest need.

Rimbaud shortly thereafter went to Paris and was swept up in the world of the Paris poets, especially Paul Verlaine. From the beginning Rimbaud's mother had questioned his writing poetry. She asked, "What can you do with it?" She questioned, "Can you make money with it?"

Since his father had left the family when Rimbaud was a small child, his strict and stern mother had been the provider. Throughout his life, he ran away from home and away from these pressures to conform to do something that would provide an income. But when he returned home there was always the questioning of his poetry.

After his disappointment with finding a male friend (if not a father figure) in Izambard, he had failed in efforts at establishing an enduring friendship with poet Paul Verlaine and later a "wild bohemian poet," Germaine Nouveau, in London. He stopped writing poetry at the age of 19, and after some passionate travels attempting a variety of jobs, he ended up trying to be a businessman as a coffee trader in Harrar in present day Ethiopia. At 37 he developed cancer of the knee, and, after unsuccessful treatments, died.

I have kept up with Alex now for 17 years and shared with him my research on the life of Arthur Rimbaud. Periodically we discuss ongoing similarities. Rimbaud became a foreman in a construction and maintenance company when he was 25. When Alex became a foreman in a construction and maintenance company at 25, I arranged to have lunch with him to point out how he was following Rimbaud's life to the year. At 31 he was a success in business as was Rimbaud at 31.

What better start could I have had? I was being encouraged by every finding, as I looked for comparable figures among Alex's friends to those in Rimbaud's group of friends. I studied every person who had known Rimbaud since his birth including all his school friends, and all the poets of Paris at the time he and Verlaine were frequenting the bars and coffee houses of Paris. I was trying to see if there were comparisons to Alex's friends or mine who were poets or artists, including students who came to the art program where I first met Alex.

Then I reasoned, if Alex were a reincarnation of Arthur Rimbaud, and I a reincarnation of Georges Izambard, then perhaps we both came back in similar teacher-student relationships in other lifetimes? What would have been those lifetimes? Were there any clues about other lifetimes in what I had found so far? The enormous sweep and power of the cyclonic energy of Arthur Rimbaud, must have come from a great leader of men in his past lives—to have all the creative power compressed in Rimbaud's brief creative period during his teens.

I lay awake at night, realizing that I was on the verge of discovering something completely new. We are spiraling down through history, coming through lifetime after lifetime, recreating similar scenes, similar personality traits, similar friendships, similar professions and goals in each new life. The soul group concept of New Age literature provided an almost perfect "family structure" model to facilitate using my genealogical research techniques to research spiritual lineages. If the student-teacher relationship that Rimbaud and Georges Izambard had was repeated in the relationship Alex and I had, then those relationships may have descended from similar student-teachers relationships earlier in history. Searching for this kind of "relationship" replication in succeeding or preceding lifetimes then became the new research tool I began working with. If Alex had a best friend in this lifetime, could he be a reincarnation of Rimbaud's best friend? Would Rimbaud's demanding and misunderstanding mother be reincarnated in Alex's life as a misunderstanding father or teacher or employer? Suddenly I realized I was not only dealing with a new key to a new kind of genealogical type spiritual research, but possibly a new key to understanding personality, psychology and history.

How dramatically all the lives of a generation of young people looking for a purpose or mission in life could be changed. What if they realized they may have soared through 86 or more previous lifetimes, gaining knowledge and experience in each one, to get here to use for their MISSION and a PURPOSE in this lifetime? If we just knew how TO REMEMBER. And if, as the New Age writers had said, each lifetime is like a classroom, and we are here to refine what we have learned in previous lifetimes, and reinterpret our message or soul group message to a new generation, advancing it yet to a higher level, then knowledge of past lives, and this journey down through time becomes essential.

I realized I was not just dealing with the life of a friend, but if there were a way I could discover what previous lifetimes Arthur Rimbaud had lived, then the origins of the energy and creativity of this outstanding poet might better be understood. When I told a poet friend of mine in New York, the potential I saw in this kind of prospect, and how I was using the techniques I had used during my lifetime of genealogical research, she said, "Your genealogical research was just a preparation. Using those techniques to develop a completely new theory of how each of us has a spiritual lineage as well as a genealogical lineage may be what you are here for." If we, in this lifetime, are returning to sites where we have been before without knowing it, how such knowledge would enrich and give meaning to our every footstep, as well as endow it with a sense of purpose, direction and history.

As I lay awake at night, my mind pondered the possibilities. I was on to something now—an adventure larger than genealogy, larger than anything before in my life. And it was just the beginning.

Lessons Learned—Chapter One

1. **We must become alert to everything that is happening around us. Everything is a clue.** All events may carry messages or meanings. We must become alert to all happenings. Recognizing that there is a "spiritual hand" in the concrete everyday world around us enables us to begin to "see in the dark." We come to understand the analogy of Plato in "The Republic," when he talks about the material things we see around us are but a shadow of realities we cannot see, realities which move us and everything around us into action. Once, when I became aware of this, I was in a video store. As I was looking at boxes of videos on the wall in front of me, one seemed to literally jump out—off the wall—*at* me and fell on the floor at my feet. It was some film about hippies in the fifties, which I never would have rented. But I picked it up and rented it. I could find nothing in the film worth seeing. But in analyzing the experience, I concluded, "Maybe this was just a test." Anyway, it was clear by then I had learned the lesson: Everything is filled with meaning.

2. **There are no accidents, no chance happenings. Coincidences are the clearest indications that spirit realities affect our lives, even guiding us when we seek to gain knowledge. Even in our human dim wits, we can recognize coincidences. And they are filled with meaning—every time.** Often when we think we are in control of our lives, we are being led. The evening I attended the showing of Agnieska Holland's *The Secret Garden*, in Ocean City, Maryland, I thought I was responding to the invitation of a friend. But little did I realize I was being led on the first phase of a journey. Seeing this film led to my seeing other films by Agnieska Holland. Eventually it led to my picking up her film on the life of Arthur Rimbaud, which started my incredible journey learning about past soul groups of which I had been a part. We are being led in this manner all the time, but we must become aware of it and open to where it leads us.

3. **I began to look at each person around me as the "current" lifetime of a spirit that had an ancient history.** If we may have lived 80 or more past lives, then each person may be just a contemporary link in a long chain of past lifetimes. Each person has within him or her an encyclopedia of knowledge, experience or skills he or she has learned and stored from past lives. Some begin using that knowledge and experience early as children. The more gifted are called prodigies. Others may unconsciously be working toward a mission in this lifetime, they had prepared for before they were born.

2

Socrates is in the
next room.

After I had seen the film about Arthur Rimbaud, and been so moved by it, I had embarked on a program of research on everything I could find about his poetry and his life. I soon realized I was searching for **preincarnations** of Alex's classmates and friends as well as my friends, to see if there was anyone around Rimbaud who might fit the personalities or life patterns of people we know now. If we all came into this lifetime with the same soul group, we had lived with before in previous lifetimes, then not only would Alex's personality have traits of Rimbaud's, but I would have those of his teacher and mentor. Some our friends, classmates, students and associates would also have been a part of Rimbaud's soul group and be identifiable by personality traits. So I began researching the lives of Rimbaud's friends, family members and fellow students. I was seeking descriptions of personality traits, work habits and accomplishments, and then searching for those same traits in people Alex and I knew. When I would find the same, I considered I had found a "match" and another past life for a member of our contemporary "soul group."

I was at the same time well underway with and continuing my "reading journey." This had started with *Many Lives, Many Masters* by Dr. Brian Weiss. This, I believe, is a watershed book. It opens the door to studies of past lives in a scientific way, which he had never considered before nor had I. His experiences seemed valid to me. His approach as a scientist appealed to me.

The occurrence of the adventure of reentering the lifetime of Arthur Rimbaud by way of my research and my growing knowledge and consciousness of him and those around him expanded my life. My mind now included knowledge of this great poet—this gift to mankind, which I had not known about before. I realized before long that my research effort to find my and Alex's friends among Rimbaud's family and friends had all the intellectual excitement of "the chase." It was like a spy thriller on television. Like genealogy, I was fitting pieces of the jigsaw puzzle together again, only this time I WAS LEARNING HISTORY, and expanding my knowledge of life and world. I also realized that I was on the path of a new kind of EDUCATION. I could have called it EDUCATION 101. This was a course whose starting place was "I." If "I" had lived in this past life as Georges Izambard, and had known Arthur Rimbaud, then I would have known his family and friends as well.

In this process of trying to find Alex's and my friends and family (as their **preincarnations** in the past), I had to study every poet in Paris at this time, who would have socialized with Rimbaud there, every childhood friend of Rimbaud and every friend of Georges Izambard. *I was doing the kind and depth of research a scholar would do for his Masters or doctoral thesis, and I was doing it as a game, and it was fun!* Perhaps most important, it was personal. I was not just seeing and studying history, I was seeing it as a part of it, from inside of it. I never would have learned this much nor have it mean as much to me, if I had studied it in a class.

I was also doing what Dr. Brian Weiss had said was what life is about: growing in knowledge and love. I was overwhelmed by the passion and intensity crammed inside Rimbaud's little body, and the incredible passion for life and painful feelings he experienced and wrote about between the ages of seven and 19. I kept thinking it is surprising he didn't just explode. When his father left the family when he was seven, he was left with a stern and demanding mother who had no appreciation of poetry—or his passion and life mission to be a poet. Consequently, he kept running away from home and trying to find someone with whom he could share his passionate feelings. Someone who would "understand." Someone he could talk to.

My continuing reading adventure had started with *Many Lives, Many Masters* and then to Dr. Brian Weiss' second book, *Through Time into Healing*. This second book had two very useful items: (1) An introduction by Raymond A. Moody, Jr., M. D., Ph.D., and (2) An Appendix which included instructions on how to make a tape to induce self-hypnosis which would allow a person to regress (venture, journey) into one's past lives. Easier said than done. I knew as soon as I read the introduction by Dr. Raymond Moody, Jr. that he was the next author on my list, as soon as I finished Dr. Brian Weiss' third book, *Only Love is Real*.

Dr. Raymond Moody had pioneered scientific research into near death experiences, which usually manifested themselves as out of body experiences. When I was a junior in college, I had become upset by instances of people using each other and being unkind and hurtful to each other. This existential sensitive concern formed at a time I was intensely studying philosophy and religion in class. One night following a particularly upsetting experience of watching one of my fraternity brothers excited about the prospect of "using" another person, I lay awake into the night, distressed by this kind of selfishness and insensitivity.

I had formed the question in my mind: "Everyone one of us will experience extreme pain in the course of our lives. Each of us will lose a mother and father, a loved one. We will have to endure illness and various forms of material deprivation. Why, then, do we hurt one another—adding to the pain the simple passage through this lifetime will require?" Unable to sleep, and tossing, I painfully struggled to find answers to these questions. Suddenly I found myself looking down, as though I were up near a corner of the ceiling of the room, peering down at my own body on the bed. Then I could see an incredible funnel seeming to go from my body up into the sky, with a bright light at the end like the sun. The feeling of love cascaded over my body in waves. And while I heard no words spoken, there was no doubt that a message was communicated to me. That message was: "I am well pleased. You are exactly on course with you life."

Soon the experience passed, but it was so exhilarating! I wanted it to continue, and I laid there for hours hoping it would. The next day I told only a few friends of this experience, since I had never heard anything like this before happening to anyone. Twenty years later, I was in Charlottesville, Virginia, where my father was a patient at the University of Virginia Hospital. One morning I picked up the local Charlottesville newspaper, and there was a large drawing of the very experience I had had. I was amazed, since I thought I was the only one in the world who had had such an experience. What I had had was a classic "out of body" experience, which had been experienced by countless thousands, who like me, had not talked about it, for fear of criticism from other people. In studies it was usually found to be a part of the Near Death Experience. I later speculated, that this would have been about the time Dr. Raymond Moody had begun his research into Near Death Experiences, and he would have been in Charlottesville. The article may have been illustrating his early findings.

I was excited by what Dr. Raymond Moody had said in the Introduction to *Through Time into Healing,* and I was eager to try my hand at self-hypnosis. I had taught psychology courses about the use of hypnosis but had never experienced it. We all have heard stories about how people are hypnotized in public and make fools out of themselves by doing silly things, which is not hypnosis at all but entertainment. So, I was eager to see how genuine hypnosis was supposed to happen. Having been reassured in the book that it was "safe," I made tapes reading out loud the format in Appendix A of Dr. Weiss' *Through Time Into Healing,* and Dr. Raymond Moody, Jr.'s book, *Coming Back, A Psychiatrist Explores Past-Life Journeys.* Some people have anxiety about entering a hypnotic state and not being able to get out of it, instead I worried, "Can I really do this?' I had no idea it would be so difficult to get thoughts of today out of your mind—to clear your mind out, so that these memories of the past lives can surface.

I reasoned with myself. I felt I had been led in the simple act of picking up a video at my local video store and watching a movie by one of my favorite filmmakers to discover a whole new world and life I had lived back in time. What in the world might come of a self induced hypnosis *intent* on journeying to a past life? At least my hope was it could give me some kind of glimpse or clue into yet another past life. With my genealogical research motor humming and ready for more action, I used this new script for self-hypnosis to try to venture back. Of course, anyone probably realizes the harder I tried the more difficult it was to relax, which was the essential ingredient. As the tape started by endlessly saying, "Relax. Relax. Relax." I tried with an increasing vengeance to relax, which, of course, made the whole thing impossible.

This means, of course, that it took many, many efforts to achieve anything near what I wanted. Finally, after weeks of trying, I was able, one evening lying down with my eyes closed listening to one of the tapes, feel like I was, in fact, floating—high in the air. As the tape continued, talking about "coming down" and looking at my feet to see what I was wearing, I realized I was looking around. I could see old the buildings around me. I was in fact (finally) seeing things.

Then I was in a house. It had a low roof, one floor, similar to houses I had seen in Florida as a child. There was an enclosed courtyard, and there was a small pool. I remember very clearly blue tiles in the pool. There were people there, and they were on the inside of the house. The next thing I remember I was inside one of the rooms, and there was a name that seemed to float...It seemed like it was in a dining room, and the name seemed to be above on a wall. It stood out in big letters. The first letters were GORG...Later I could clearly remember the first four letters, but had trouble with the last three which did not seem familiar. Was it Gorgoyle? Or Gorgon? No, these didn't sound right. Then, I heard a commotion, and someone said, "Socrates is in the next room."

I knew then both where I was and what time in history it was. I was in Classical Greece, somewhere before 399 B.C. I was at an event where Socrates was present, and I assumed I was in Athens, Greece. That was pretty much all of the "remembering" of this past event. It did seem before and after this event, I had been high up (perhaps at the entrance of the Acropolis?) looking toward the sea. It was sunrise or sunset, and clouds that spread out over the sky were red. And there was the feeling of extreme peace and calm.

The next day I could not wait to get to the library to see if I could find somebody by the name of GORG...I picked up an Encyclopedia of Classical Greece, and looked down the index, and there it was! The name I had felt emblazoned across the room in the house where I was in my self-hypnosis, was GORGIAS. I had never read nor heard about a Gorgias, so I was eager to know who he was. If he lived at the same time as Socrates, and would have known him, this would have been an extremely positive support for my thesis and that I was on the right track. And finally would he have been at an event where Socrates would have been in the next room?

I had gotten to the library as fast as I could. Unlike college days, where going to the library to study was often something I dreaded or found to be tedious work, the library had now become a gold mine of adventure. Books now held hidden chambers of discoveries. The library had answers, secrets, information that was opening up the key to my past—a past now stretching back not just a century before but 2,400 years before! Soon I found that Gorgias was a sophist and a teacher of rhetoric. Not only did he know Socrates, one's of Plato's dialogues bears his name! In the dialogue GORGIAS, Socrates appears with Gorgias and some of Gorgias' followers. If I had been in a house full of people, possibly the home of Gorgias, who knew Socrates, who would I have been?

By now I was developing the idea, that while hypnosis may be a good way to "remember" events, incidents and persons from past lives, it is certainly not the only way. If traumatic death events from past lives, buried in our subconscious, result in our having phobias in our current lifetime as Dr. Weiss proposed, then, I reasoned, why can't positive and happy memories from our past intrude into our conscious minds as well? I had observed that everyone had favorite periods of history above other periods. Why? Why weren't they all the same? I began to develop the theory that our favorite periods in history are favorites because we harbor repressed memories of happy, productive or fulfilling past lives during that period. We are "into"—favorite periods and/or places because subconsciously *we remember*. We choose to read about these places or times in history books or novels, go see plays about or visit them on vacations because we have invested time in past lives, memories of which we still retain in our subconscious. And likewise, we could be attracted to a period of history because it was particularly difficult, and we had died with issues unresolved or missions unfulfilled, and our preoccupation with the period, is an attraction to a lifetime we felt that had not been completed.

I grew up in Georgia, where battles during the Civil War raged the full length of the state—from Chickamauga in the northwest extreme part of the state to Savannah in the southeast—destroying Atlanta in this path. That was nearly 150 years ago, when Atlanta only had 10,000 to 13,000 people in it, and today passions in the state are still high. Why is that? Why do thousands of reenactors don their Confederate and Union uniforms and fight those battles, over and over and over, on the same battleground sites where hundreds and thousands fell dead during the Civil War?

I spoke to one of these reenactors several years ago, proposing that in a previous lifetime these reenactors were those very soldiers who fought and died there. "They are still fighting in this lifetime because they are unable to accept the results of those battles in history," I said. In this lifetime they take to those battlefields once more, reenacting, reliving the unresolved ends to their past "life as a soldier in the Civil War." After a long pause he agreed with my statement. Then he said, "You know at a reenactment in Tennessee where my great-grandfather died, they once took a count and realized that they had exactly the same number of reenactors as there had been casualties in that battle during the war. These may have been the same soldiers to the man."

Then I began to test my theory on myself. I focused on the images I had seen under my own self-hypnosis. If I were "remembering" an event where I was present, where Socrates and Gorgias were present, an event in ancient Greece, then this should have been a part of my past—in a previous lifetime. Had there been anything in my favorite places, events or time in history to support this? Then I remembered.

My brother had persuaded my father to buy the Encyclopedia Britannica for the family's use, saying how he and I could use it in school. But it would be I who was to become the main beneficiary. I suffered from sinus trouble a lot, and in the first grade I was out of school for six weeks with measles and whooping cough. When I was home sick, I would pour through the encyclopedia reading through the volumes and studying things that interested me. No later than seven I had focused on my favorite picture. It was a drawing of the Acropolis.

My father had a business on the north end of Hamilton Street in Dalton, and if one stood in the middle of the street and looked north, he would face Mount Rachel, the highest hill of the city. It was topped by a water tank, which supplied the city the water, and a large neon star. The star was lighted during the Christmas season each year and could be seen from throughout the town.

But what I saw through my seven-year-old eyes was that its shape and proportions appeared identical with those of the Acropolis. With a little trimming here and there a modern day Propylaea and Parthenon could be reconstructed and fit nicely there, overlooking and overwhelming my hometown of Dalton, Georgia, the way the Acropolis had done in Athens, Greece 2,500 years before. I don't remember discussing this with anyone at the time, but I do remember my drawings and blueprints of my dreams at home when I was alone. While others boys at seven and eight were out playing baseball and football, I was drawing blueprints of my dream to reconstruct the Acropolis in north Georgia.

On Confederate Memorial Day in Miss Eugenia Sapp's second grade class at City Park School, we twisted metal coat hangers to make them round a made a wreath. After we walked single-file to Westview Cemetery, we took our wreaths and placed them on the graves of the

Confederate dead along with little Confederate flags. The back row was not forgotten, and there wreaths and four American flags placed on the graves of four union soldiers who lost their lives in battle. After school that day, when my classmates were playing baseball or going to the movies, I went home to study my latest plans for the Acropolis on Mt. Rachel. My seven year old mind thought, what a shame the town carries the name Dalton. Maybe we could call it New Athens (we couldn't rename it Athens, because Georgia already had one—where the state university was, and where I would spend four years as an undergraduate).

When I became a student at the University of Georgia in Athens, I made A's in everything about Classical Culture—Greece and Rome. This included philosophy where I studied Plato, where I also always made A's. I came to believe that academic interest and success in certain areas are clues to success and experience in these areas in previous lifetimes. We are attracted to, interested in and have academic success in a subject, because of our experience in some way with it in the past. This would mean we are born with "memories" of these successes and are comfortable with them. We excel in them building on past successes.

Were there any other interests to support this idea of my having lived in Ancient Greece? There were indeed. When I had returned to Georgia to try to use the farm as an arts center, what name would I choose? There was NEVER any question, I would choose the name "Academy", and apply it to Georgia. But why Academy? Again, I turned to the Encyclopedia Britannica, and pointed out that our Georgia Fine Arts Academy would be modeled after the Academy of Plato, which also was founded outside the metropolis of the time—Athens. Our Academy would likewise be founded in an old historic "grove" outside the metropolis—our metropolis being Atlanta. Here, the arts would be taught, but an environment created with teachers from all over the world. Students would not only learn art, but they would expand their knowledge of the world they lived in.

At this point, I was seeing a trend, a steady consistent logical pattern of reaffirmations of my interest in Classical Greece. If I were in that house with Socrates and Gorgias, then who would I have been in that lifetime. I studied how Plato had fled Athens following the death of his friend Socrates, had gone on his own educational odyssey around the Mediterrean before he returned home. He had traveled the same amount of time my own educational odyssey had taken—12 years. He had returned after his educational odyssey and founded the original Academy. When I realized I was following the schedule of his lifetime to the year, it became too heady for me, and too grandiose, so I put that possibility on a shelf.

With the possibility of having lived in Athens, Greece at the time Plato's dialogues were being written, I plunged into studying Plato's dialogues and everything I could read about his life. I learned more about Plato, the history of Classical Greece and Classical Greek Philosophy in a couple of weeks than I had learned in all the philosophy courses I had taken in college. It didn't take me long to realize that I was "reeducating" myself, starting with my favorite subject (and all of our favorite subjects)—"I". After losing myself (my present self) by immersing myself in the life, times and world of Arthur Rimbaud, I was now on a second "back-in-time" journey of discovery. I was now back in time (in my research) to Classical Greece—learning about philosophy, history, Greek drama, the arts, and the process of trying to find who I was and who was in my soul group then? No doubt, the patterns of my own conscious, waking interests and passions, as well as my one successful effort at self-hynosis, were telling me that the Acropolis, Plato's dialogues, Athens, and Plato's Academy were all a part of it.

I began by studying the life of Plato and what Athens was like when he lived there. He lived from 428–347 B. C. I was surprised to read that his real name was Aristocles. He was a highly successful wrestler and had been given the nickname (a ring name) of Plato. "Plato" was the Greek word for "Broad," a name his fans shouted when he wrestled because of his "broad" shoulders. He used his nickname (his ring name) as his pen name when he later began writing. He was the son of well-to-do parents with many political and social connections, so he considered becoming a playwright, a wrestler, or going into politics. He had even won the wrestling prize at the Isthmian Games, but was not interested enough to pursue it by competing in the Olympic Games at Olympia.

Like many young people today, he could not decide what he wanted to do with his life. While still considering all of his options, he joined some of his friends, who would listen to Socrates, a wise and learned man, who had attracted a following of young men who were fascinated by his philosophical questioning. He taught by asking questions to those who listened to him. Socrates was interested in what constituted a "good" life, and his teachings had such a ring of truth, that a following had developed, and Plato became a part of that group of young questioning Athenians.

Plato followed Socrates with his friends, listening and learning from their mentor for nine years. When a group of tyrants took over Athens, and proceeded to silence those who taught their followers to think, Socrates was tried and sentenced to death in 399 B. C. In fear that he would be implicated with Socrates, Plato fled and began his twelve year odyssey throughout the Mediterranean.

As I read Plato's Dialogues, particularly *Phaedo* and the *Phaedrus*, I was fascinated to learn that they too, believed in past and future lives, as a matter of course. Plato proposed that all learning was remembering. As I read this I realized that I had stumbled onto this track of thinking myself. Or, perhaps as Socrates said, that was I just remembering.

Plato's life was not all that of a quiet scholar or pedagogue, spending life confined to the library stacks doing research or writing down the accounts of Socrates' dialogues with his young followers. Twice Plato had had to flee for his life, and once he had been sold into slavery. After leaving Athens fearful that he would be punished for being aligned with Socrates, as a part of his "educational odyssey," Plato traveled to the court of Dionysius I in Syracuse in 388 B. C. He found that his opinions fell into a great disfavor, and he was deported on a Spartan vessel and marked for sale on the slave block in Aegina. There Anniceris rescued him by negotiating a price with the auctioneer.

Later, in 367 B. C., when Dionysius II succeeded his father as dictator, his uncle, Dion, was in charge of his education, and entrusted it to Plato, after he had come to Syracuse in Sicily a second time. This time Plato was accused of plotting his student's demise when he attempted to teach Dionysius II his model of the philosopher-king. So, again Plato was forced to flee. Once he fled from Athens when Socrates died, and now he had to flee twice from Syracuse. "Fleeing for your life" was a part of Plato's early turbulent life.

In spite of these stressful ordeals, Plato took advantage of his travels, and his "educational odyssey" included travelling to Megara, on the isthmus of Corinth, where he studied geometry under his friend Euclid, whom we consider the father of geometry. He is reported to have gone to Egypt to study astronomy and settled in Cyrene, a city of north Africa, to study mathematics with the teacher Theodorus. He spent some time in Tarentum in southern Italy, where Archytas, a famous mathematician and follower of Pythagoras, was mayor.

I reflected on my own "educational odyssey," which included studying at Yale under H. Richard Niebuhr, the foremost Christian ethicist of the century, who, during our daily morning coffees in the Common Room, would regularly ask my opinion on the Civil Rights Movement, which was then raging across the South. We loved noted Church Historian Kenneth Scott Latourette, whom we called "Uncle Ken", well into his 80's. And studying at Yale gave me the opportunity to meet my intellectual hero, Paul Tillich, who was on the faculty at Harvard but was visiting Yale at the time.

One memorable Sunday, after he had preached the sermon in Dwight Chapel on the main Yale quadrangle, I stood in line, like a fan at a rock concert to meet my "hero." I thanked him for what he had meant to me, and tried to explain that it was his kind of thinking that had brought me to the Ivy League to continue my education. "I wanted to be where this kind of thinking was taking place." It was his book, *Theology of Culture,* that had become a manual for my future efforts to develop an arts center, and help young artists realize that they were carriers of and responsible for "divine messages" which the arts embody.

And at Yale I had had the opportunity to hear leading theologians, church historians and Biblical scholars from around the world. When I was studying at Oxford, I had met Werner Pelz, who had written *God is No More*, a book sweeping Britain at the time. It may have appeared controversial, but in essence it seemed to be saying if we but "love" others we are freed from attacking them because they do not "believe" the way we do.

The more I studied about Plato, I wondered why had I never studied more in college about the life of this man who was to transform Western Philosophy? He was an adventurer in a way that makes our lives look bland. And while he was a recorder of what his mentor and friend Socrates had said in groups while discussing philosophical questions, no doubt Plato had, in the later dialogues, added some of his own interpretations and views.

I had been most interested in his dialogue entitled *Phaedo*. In it he discussed the concept of learning by remembering, and restates Socrates' belief that we have lived before and will live again, making the soul immortal. When I read this, I felt like I was on the path, my path, of where I was going with my reading journey, and my newly found game, I was now calling "spiritual lineaging." I was using genealogical research techniques I had used for years in genealogical research, except now I was using them to research the historical path of our immortal souls. It was a course of being born, living a lifetime, dying and being born again. In each lifetime our spirits are responsible, individually and as part of a soul group—charged with a mission of making this world better, in whatever way is our mission to do it.

My excitement was growing. If each of us is an immortal soul, housed in successive bodies down through history, then that means we are but temporary dwellers in our body in one lifetime. We have lived before, and we will live again. *Death then just becomes a nap between lifetimes.* Or death is just exchanging one body for another one and starting over to continue our missions.

Being a historian, I realized how this realization, if generally accepted could change entirely the way we look at life. I had been told that Albert Einstein had read the book *Flatland,* by Edwin A. Abbot at least once annually. It deals with other dimensions above and below, what we experience. If we are indeed an immortal soul, which takes residence in one body at a time, this means we could have had 80 lifetimes (like the case study in Dr. Brian Weiss's *Many Lives, Many Masters*) or more, and we could have an infinite number in the future. And if we have an individual and group mission in each lifetime—a mission or message to refine, reinterpret or advance in each of those lifetimes, then how important it would be to have knowledge of those past lifetimes—to know where we are going and that we are "on a mission."

In pulling back and seeing history through the eyes of geologists, astronomers, anthropologists and historians, and if we view history as an evolving process in which each of us is growing in knowledge and love, then I began to see our lives as GOD'S THUNDERBOLTS HURLED THROUGH TIME. We need to learn how to see ourselves standing in the vertical line of history—to think vertically in time. If we are learning and gaining and storing knowledge in each generation, expanding our consciousness then our knowledge of our past lives and role in soul groups now becomes crucial.

My research continued. If I had been at the home of Gorgias, with Socrates present, then I would have known others of the time. Since, I had started my journey with a focus on Alex, and the possibility that he would have been Arthur Rimbaud in a past lifetime, who in the company of Socrates and Gorgias, might he have been then? So, I began to look through the dialogues. The best of these concerning personalities of the times was the dialogue *Symposium,* where persons in Plato's and Socrates's world were attending a banquet and where they were asked to give speeches about what they thought was the meaning of love.

Among the guests at that dinner party, I began to see the traits I was looking for, the traits of my former student and friend, Alex and the explosive personality of the young Arthur Rimbaud. They were alive and well in Alcibiades!

LESSONS LEARNED—CHAPTER TWO

1. **Where you are now living is a clue.** Study the history of the town or region where you live. You may have returned to continue an individual mission or soul group mission that you had begun before where you live now, or you may have lived there for a short time in a previous lifetime. Is there any history connected with your hometown or state that you are enthralled with? Is there any individual person in history there with whom you identify with? (You may have been that person, close to that person, family member of that person, or known him or her well.)

2. **Study the periods of history that attract you.** Do you read books or go see movies that deal with a particular period of time that is your favorite. It may be your favorite because you lived in it, and it evokes strong memories and sentiments from you past (repressed) memories.

3. **Are there places you dream to visit, and want to go on a vacation.** These dreams are clues. You may be attracted to a place because of your having been there in a past life.

4. **Daydreams are clues.** Do you have fantasies about building a place, living in a place? Do you have fantasies about being an important person—wealthy, military figure, writer, painter, etc.? This may be a clue to a past life where you achieved fame or recognition.

5. **Do you have recurring night dreams?** Analyze these carefully. They may be filled with clues, in that you may be remembering scenes or events from a past life.

6. **Whom would you choose to be,** if you were to go to a Halloween Party or Costume Ball, or have any occasion to dress in costume as another person? What period of history would you choose? These choices, and all choices, should be seen as clues of whom you may

have been in a past lifetime. We are "remembering" all the time without realizing it.

3

They love, and hate, and cannot do without him.

If there was a cavalier, a swashbuckler, an *enfant terrible* in the group surrounding Socrates that would correspond to Arthur Rimbaud, it was clearly Alcibiades. He was born about 450 B. C. and died in 404 B. C. I had been looking for a precursor to the flamboyance which Rimbaud depicted when he arrived in Paris mocking the established poets. Agnieska Holland had pictured Rimbaud in his brash 15th year arrogantly up on top of a table walking down it at a Parisian poets' gathering, kicking food and plates into the laps of those gathered for a reading, describing them as bourgeois.

I had discovered Alcibiades while reading Plato's Dialogues. When I got to *Symposium,* I found it filled with people who would have been close friends of Plato, and well known by him. The name "symposium" was given to a regular all-male dinner gathering of friends, but this one was special. This was a banquet at Agathon's house in 416 B. C. A few days before Agathon, a handsome young tragic poet, then about 31, had won his first "victory" prize at the dramatic competition of tragic plays as part of the Festival of Dionysus. This was held at the Theatre of Dionysus, a theatre at the foot of the Acropolis, which accommodated about 30,000 people. So, it was a kind of celebration attended by friends.

The gist of the dialogue is that each one was asked by the host to make a speech on what he thought was the true meaning of love. The roster of guests was a wonderful clue in my search for this earlier soul group, though not all of them were necessarily a part of it. Attending the banquet and making speeches were:

Socrates, who was then 53.

Pausanias, a disciple of Prodicos, the Sophist, of Ceos.

Aristophanes, the famous comic poet, then about 32. In his comedy, *Clouds*, performed five years earlier, he had made fun of Socrates. *Clouds* took place at a home next to Plato's Academy, and Socrates was pictured as floating above them. At the performance, in the grand gesture of a good sport, Socrates had stood up during the play, while he was being depicted on stage, so the audience could compare the likeness of the actor portraying him to the real thing.

Alcibiades, then about 35, made a speech at the banquet praising Socrates. Alcibiades had saved Socrates' life in a battle once, and in another battle had his life saved by Socrates in return.

The story of the banquet was told by Aristodemos, who attended it with Socrates, but the dialogue is retold by Apollodorus to a friend while they were walking 15 years later. Apollodorus is also described in the dialogue *Phaedo*, weeping at the time of the death of Socrates.

When I read the description of the arrival of Alciabides at the banquet, how he was drinking, and talking to the others present, the picture from the film about Rimbaud jumping on the table at the gathering of Parisian poets filled my mind.

I then began to read about Alcibiades in the Encyclopedia Britannica. Here indeed was the energy of a young Rimbaud along with his dramatic flare. I found a biography of Alcibiades at the local library, but marveled at the description of him by Plutarch. In reading Plutarch's biography, I also marveled at Plutarch himself. How wonderful it is that we have this incredible group of biographies—what a great contribution Plutarch made to expand and preserve our knowledge of history!

I began to study these lives now taking their place in a spiritual lineage, starting with someone I knew in the present. Starting with Rimbaud, I was now studying his past life as Alcibiades. I began to feel all the excitement I had felt in my genealogical research, when I would develop a theoretical scenario and then test it with the facts of my research as I would uncover them.

In this case, I was seeking to find:

1. Similar or the same personality traits.

2. Similar or the same profession, e. g., writer, teacher, orator.

3. Accomplishments in a successive lifetime that would refine, reinterpret, test or continue a mission started in a previous lifetime.

4. Be a part of a soul group that would also be coming down from life to life, including having a larger soul group mission or purpose.

With this in mind, as I read about Alcibiades, especially in Plutarch, I was amazed at his energy, his intrigues, the power of his *presence*. Also, flashing in my mind were stories I had read about the life of Alexander the Great. Some years earlier I had read all the historical novels of Mary Renault. She had written fictional novels, based on her own historical research, of this very period in history. She presented pictures of the periods of these major historical figures by describing each one as seen through the eyes of fictional bystanders. Her fictional weaving of some of the stories gave you a feeling of the atmosphere of the times. Sometimes she made you feel like she knew the historical figures themselves, by adding details and depths, which I assumed must be fictional at the time I read them. I now found my line of research making me question how fictional her accounts were. Now I was thinking, "Perhaps these details were not so fictional. Perhaps Mary Renault was there in a previous lifetime. Perhaps she was one of those fictional bystanders in a previous lifetime. Perhaps now in her novel she is simply *remembering* the detail and recording it in her stories about historical persons she knew and historical events she witnessed."

Among her novels were: *Fire From Heaven*, about the early years of Alexander the Great, and *The Persian Boy* about the later years of Alexander the Great. Images of Alexander kept flashing in my mind as I began to see incredible similarities. I paused reading about Alcibiades and started reading about Alexander, looking for the similarities. They were many, and they were profound. At one point, when I was reading from Plutarch about Alcibiades, I had to look up at the name at the top of the page, because I thought I was reading about Alexander by mistake.

Very, very quickly, I began to make a strong case that Alexander the Great was a reincarnation of Alcibiades. Alcibiades had been murdered in Phrygia in 404 B. C., and Alexander had been born 48 years later in 356 B. C.

There was an incredible section in Plutarch describing Alcibiades in battle that could have been lifted directly from Alexander's advance into Persia. Here you see all the charisma of Alexander (and Rimbaud) in the descriptions of Alcibiades.

In one case the soldiers who followed Alcibiades in one of his battles were so exalted in their feelings of success, and felt such a degree of pride, that they looked upon themselves as invincible. They refused to mix with other soldiers who had been a part of their success. At one point they refused to exercise with them. When a trophy was raised by Ephesians to the disgrace of the Athenians, the next day Alcibiades erected his own trophy and proceeded to lay waste the whole province. No one attempted to resist him. This also could have been taken straight out of Alexander's campaign into Persia. Like Alexander, when Alcibiades approached the Bithynaians they were so terrified that they gave him booty and entered into an alliance with him. He won everyone over by his use of Spartan techniques. This Alexander did with the Persians. Like Alexander in one naval battle, Alcibiades forced the sailors to disembark, and then pursued and slaughtered them. The Athenians took all their ships and the spoils that went with them. I wondered, "How is it that here is someone so very much like Alexander, that I learned so little about in my history classes?"

As I proceeded to learn about Alcibiades, I saw more similarities of Alexander and Rimbaud emerge. Like Rimbaud, Alciabiades had been left without a father when he was a child—Alciabiades' father, who was in command of the Athenian army, was killed at Coronea, Boeotia, when he was four. Rimbaud's father had left the family when Rimbaud was seven. Alcibiades was well-born and wealthy, and when his father died, his guardian became the statesman Pericles, a distant relation. But Pericles was too concerned with his own political leadership to give Alcibiades much attention.

As he grew up, Alcibiades was strikingly handsome and very bright, but he was extravagant, irresponsible and self-centered. Despite these attributes he had been attracted to Socrates, whose moral strength and keen mind was like a magnet to young students all over Athens. Socrates was also attracted to Alcibiades, in whom he saw great intellectual promise.

Ironically, they both served together in the army at Potidaea (432 B. C.), where Alcibiades was defended by Socrates when he was wounded. And the situation was reversed in the Battle of Delium (424 B. C.), north of Athens, when Alcibiades protected Socrates in a military retreat. This was described by Plutarch.

In Athens all young men attended the gymnasium during their teens until they were 18, when they served in the army for two years. Alcibiades was descibed as being very young, so he was probably 18 when he was a soldier in the battle against Potidaea. Socrates was lodged in the same tent and stood next to him in battle. In one battle, where they both performed with bravery, and while Alcibiades was receiving a wound, Socrates placed himself in front of him and without question saved him. Later, in the battle of Delium, the Athenians were routed, and Alcibiades, on horseback, stayed to shelter Socrates from danger and brought him home to safety despite the fact that the enemy was threatening to cut them off on all sides.

Alcibiades as a child was flamboyant as Alexander was as a child. Stories of his childhood could compare to Alexander or Arthur Rimbaud. For example, once being hard pressed in wrestling, and fearing to be thrown, he got the hand of his antagonist to his mouth, and bit it with all his force; and when the other loosed his hold presently, and said, "You bite, Alcibiades, like a woman." Alcibiades replied, "No, like a lion."

Another time he was playing dice, and a cart came down the road. He called and asked the driver to allow him to throw, but the driver ignored him. So brash was Alcibiades, that he lay down in the front of the cart, which terrified the driver as well as his friends. But he stopped the cart.

When he was past his childhood, he went once to a grammar school, and asked the master for one of Homer's books. When the master answered that he had nothing of Homer's, Alcibiades gave him a blow with his fist and left.

Once while playing a game with friends, he agreed with his companions to give a box on the ear to Hipponicus, the father of Callias, whose birth and wealth made him a person of great influence and repute. People were justly offended at his insolence, and it became known throughout the city. Early the next morning, Alcibiades went to the house of Hipponicus and knocked on his door. When he was let in he took off his garments, and presenting his naked body to Hipponicus asking him to scourge and chastise him as he pleased. Upon this Hipponicus forgot all his resentment and not only pardoned him, but soon after gave him his daughter Hipparete in marriage.

And so Alcibiades' good looks and his pleasing manner enabled him to charm most everyone. These were matched by his dramatic flare, with which he overwhelmed people by doing the unexpected. This dramatic flare later extended into his role as military leader as well and caused men to follow him wherever he led. This same public charisma was duplicated almost exactly in Alexander the Great.

By now, I had developed the theory that if we knew our spiritual pre-incarnations, we could "remember" as Plato would say, talents and abilities from the past. My research was leading me to suspect that we may be born with repressed memories of skills that may have been taught over years in a previous lifetime. When someone says, "He has a knack or aptitude for.........", it may be that our knack or skills are the result of hard work learned in a lifetime before, skills that we are ready to use now.

I had another favorite period in history that began to blossom in middle school. This was a love and fascination for a single period in Egyptian history—that period surrounding Amenhotep IV, who became known as Ikhnaton. When he became Pharoah, he caused a revolution by overnight changing the state religion to the worship of a monotheistic concept of God. Virtually the entire priestly class of the existing religion was out of a job, and this is probably one of the best ways to cause a revolution.

My brother had a book entitled *The Egyptian*," by Mika Waltari, which was about this revolutionary pharoah, who died c. 1362 B. C. A movie was later made from the book. While I know my interest in Ikhnaton may have been caused by my own emerging interest in religion, and my desire to spend my life "helping other people," I was struck by the fact that virtually no other period of Egyptian history interested me at all. Even when I had studied Ancient History, while an undergraduate at the University of Georgia, the chapter about Ikhnaton has the only pages in the textbooks that remain underlined with comments down the margins, to this day.

Why then this "personal" preoccupation with this one period of Egyptian history and no other? I had been puzzled by this even before I began to explore Brian Weiss's discussions of reincarnation. Now a possibility was growing stronger. Suppose our preferences to history and places emerge straight out of our repressed memory of having lived then or having been there?

While exploring the past of Alcibiades, I had also started studying Amenhotep IV—whom my brother seemed equally interested in. Could this mean he and I both were in this "Egyptian soul group." After months of research into this "soul group", I had come to see similarities between some of my brother's personality traits and those of Ikhnaton. When I started looking for my own, I had found them in his father, Amenhotep III.

Continuing my study of these ancient families, I continued to look at this prominent line of flamboyant personalities—Arthur Rimbaud, Alcibiades, and Alexander the Great. Meanwhile, my friend, Alex, was showing some very pronounced compulsive behavior as he began moving through his early twenties. Not only had he been reading in the occult, following the pattern of Rimbaud, but his best work of art, which I later persuaded him to give to me, was "The Birth of Dionysus." This piece, which he did in New York, showed Dionysus as a full blown adult, hurtling out of the side of Zeus. Zeus was endowed with all his manly virtues, and in two panels on either side were voluptuous nymphs.

His other art work, which was moved to his new apartment, when he left New York, became supplemented by newer pieces, which in turn were exhibited as part of a huge annual event—the Rites of Spring. This spring festival, which took months of planning—starting during the fall of the previous year—was as lavish as Alex could make it. The cost of the refreshments, the incredible decorations, and the entertainment, took far more money than he could afford. Seeing the passion which drove him, friends chipped in and gave money to help and volunteered to serve the food and drinks.

I soon realized we were seeing something here very primitive and ancient. It was a "rite" which I began to realize resulted from a deep seated memory in a past life. It was a full blown organized festival, which one person was trying to put on. He had done this before—in a past lifetime. I had absolutely no doubt. Not only had he done it before, it had been a monstrous event—huge in its proportions and effect. I speculated that it affected a whole city or whole country. This event was in no way connected with making money, the opposite. It was in no way intended to further his career or reputation. Alex was doing this because he had to. Like the compulsion of the artist, he did it because "he must." In my arts classes, I had talked about the artist who paints, "because he must."

My next step was to begin searching for someone in the soul group of Amenhotep III and Amenhotep IV (Ikhanaton), who would have been a preincarnation of Alcibiades and Alexander the Great. I soon found him. His name was Yuya, and he was the father-in-law of Amenhotep III, who ruled 1417–1379 B. C. Yuya was Officiate at the Temple of Min, and Lt. General of the Charioteers. Immediately I saw manifestations of Yuya in both Alex and Alcibiades.

Alex compulsively and ceremoniously worked up to six months each year making preparations for his annual Rites of Spring. The happiest I ever saw him was when he was planning for this annual festival. That he was reliving and continuing the kinds of preparation he would have been doing as the Officiate of the Temple of Min is one of the best explanations I can imagine for his fever of excited preparations. I know of no one else with such an annual passion for an event like this, which is so out of step with the present. Min was an Egyptian god of fertility, and the annual spring event that Alex worked toward reflected the themes and functions of this ancient festival.

Then I read about a major event in the life of Alcibiades which could best be explained by his living a former lifetime as Yuya. Early in his life, Alcibiades caught the attention of his fellow Athenians at the Olympic Games. Again, Plutarch described it best. My mind was switching back and forth between Alcibiades and Yuya, Lt. General of the Charioteers in Egypt from 1417 to 1379 B. C., as I read it.

Alcibiades' expenses in horses kept for the public games, and in the number of his chariots, were matter of great observation. He was the only person—never did any one else either an individual or the king, send seven chariots to the Olympic games. As Thucydides says, he at once won the first, the second, and the fourth prize, and even also the third, as Euripides relates it. He outdid every distinction that ever was known or thought of in that kind.

The emulation displayed by the representatives of various states in the presents which they made to him, made his success even more illustrious. The Ephesians erected a magnificently adorned tent for him. The city of Chios furnished him with provisions for his horses and with great numbers of beasts for sacrifice. The inhabitants of Lesbos sent him wine and other provisions for his entertainment.

As I read these remarks and began to accumulate support for the notion that Alex stood in the spiritual lineage of Yuya, Alcibiades, Alexander the Great, and Arthur Rimbaud, I began to speculate on how spectacular it would be, if each of us could somehow remember our past lives. Knowledge of and the study of our past lives could add to our strengths and hopefully our self-confidence, if we just knew how to remember.

My own experience in certain areas, suggested that we are aided in enterprises in which we have the support of what New Age writers call spirit guides, and events are orchestrated to push us along. The writing of this book, for example, as is all art, according to Socrates in Plato's dialogue *Ion,* is a case where the artist or writer is but an instrument, an agent, in a work of art. That art Socrates contends in *Ion* is but a vehicle for a divine message or divine messages. It is the muses or spirits, according to Socrates, who write with our hands. It is better for the artist to become "mad,' than egotistical, to empty our minds of our own thoughts and ideas, so that "divine message" are free to come through us.

Yesterday, while I paused in my writing and research about Yuya and Alexander the Great, I got up and turned on the television set, only to remember that the cable had gone out. Wanting a break, I was frustrated, and went to the cabinet to pick out some past video tape, to serve as a restful break. As I opened the cabinet, I began to think, "Wait, could it be that the cable being out is but an opportunity to be led by what Brian Weiss calls the Master Spirits. Perhaps I am supposed to pick out a tape they want me to watch instead of the mindless programming I might normally see on television during this time of day?"

Sure enough, I put my hand on a tape and turned it around to see "Min" written on it. Min was the Eyptian god for whom Yuya was the high priest, and the officiate at his temple. When I put it into the VCR, I remembered that I had taped it some years before because it was a special on Egypt, dealing with the lifetimes of Amenhotep III and Amenhotep IV. It talked about the Temple of Min, and how inhabitants in that town are still celebrating spring festivals (like the one Alex had been planning and celebrating and was planning as I wrote). The festivals, starting with Min, had come down through successive religions to the present day.

It was followed by a program on Alexandria which describing how one of the mosques there was considered the burial place of Alexander the Great. I had taped this, and I had seen this before, several years before, but having just written about Alexander the Great a few minutes earlier, and feeling "guided" to walk to this tape due to the circumstances of the cable on my television set being out, I was feeling chill bumps as I watched it. I really did not remember the narrator descending a ladder going deep down into the burial vault of this mosque in Alexandria, and there at the bottom was what was believed to be the remains, the burial place, of Alexander the Great. There was no questioning of my feelings. I felt reverence and awe and deep respect for this life brought to an end here in Alexandria.

I was filled with the realization of how this discovery of the "spiritual lineage" that each of us has, can connect us with, and personalize, history in a way it never had before. This scene which had been nothing but a two dimensional, academic, semi-boring, detached tour guide lecture, when I taped it, was now explosive with meaning and feeling. This history had become personal. I later came to believe in my research, that Alexander the Great was a man I knew in a previous lifetime, and was very close to—a personal friend about whom I had cared deeply, as well as knowing those who had known him.

In my readings of New Age books on my reading journey I had already come to realize:

1. We are living in a "messages being sent" world. Messages, such as this one, are being sent to us all the time—through other people, through scenes in movies or on television, in books that we are reading. Frequently we call this a "coincidence," when we are thinking something and then it happens, or we see something, and five minutes later somebody mentions it again in a different context.

2. Events are being incredibly orchestrated. When Shakespeare said "all the world's a stage," he must surely have been conscious of this in his own experience. Sometimes, when events didn't work out as I had planned or thought they would, I realized I was being slowed down until somebody else in my life caught up with me, so that certain events would turn out right. We are standing in a kind of experiential beam. I would tell my students in the arts program, "when we are doing exactly what we are supposed to be doing with our lives, then we are standing our beam." If you are standing in your beam, it is like floating down a river <u>with</u> the current, but when you are not standing in your beam, it is like swimming upstream <u>against</u> the current. There are times when I have, within a given day, crossed through my beam—out, then in, then out again—and I could feel it each time. By this I mean, when I am doing the "right" thing for me, what I am here to do, and supposed to be doing, I can feel almost a lift or boost in the direction I'm going. When I'm wasting time, or not realizing my potential, or do something wasteful, I feel a kind of malaise. So, within a given day, you can experience each of these at different times. What we should learn to do is analyze our feelings, and learn how to move into our beams.

As I write this, it is April 1, 2001, Sunday night, and Alex's annual Rites of Spring party is just now winding down. It started at 5 p.m. on Friday. The revelers have gone through two days and nights without sleep. Unknowingly they are celebrating an event at least 3,300 years old which is still being celebrated in its place of origin—Egypt. But what they don't know in Alexandria is that the spirit of their namesake is alive and well and living in Atlanta, Georgia. Two nights ago, when I was there at his annual spring festival, I could pick out, by their Macedonian names in history, Alex's friends from his soul group in that lifetime. To this day I call Alex's friends by Alexander the Great's name for them: his "Royal Bodyguards" and "Royal Companions." When I don't get to one of his parties I ask, "Were your Royal Bodyguards, your Royal Companions, there?" I was to learn in future research that Andre Breton, Alex in his most recent past lifetime, would, in a similar way to

Alexander the Great's Royal Bodyguards and Royal Companions, gather artists around him in Paris during the Surrealist Period of art.

If we live 80 lifetimes or a hundred or more, every one cannot be like Alexander the Great's. It may be that the soul group's accomplishments rather than the individual's are more important in a given lifetime. I hope that a growing consciousness and awareness of who we are, and who we have been down through the ages, as a living conscious spiritual entity, will help us rise to the occasion of recognizing and fulfilling our purpose and mission in this lifetime and those to come.

LESSONS LEARNED—CHAPTER THREE

1. **It is a clue to find a person exhibiting odd or unusual personality traits** that do not conform to behavior expected of him or her. When we view an individual not just in terms of his or her genetic parents or grandparents, but view their interests and personality as resulting from a repressed memory of 80 past lifetimes or more, then that gives us a whole new and different perspective. I have wonderful friends in New York, who have a daughter who has become a flamenco dancer and flies back and forth to Madrid. Her grandfather was a Jewish rabbi from Little Rock, and she grew up in Georgia. There is nothing in her family history or her individual past which would explain her interest and the course she has taken in this lifetime. In discussions I have had with her mother, she confesses that the idea of past lives is the most rational explanation.

2. **We may choose a lifetime in terms of what we can learn from it.** One writer has proposed that we view each lifetime as a classroom experience. We are here to learn. This again explains why we choose our parents, place of birth—on the basis of the extent to which we can continue our life or soul group mission. If we have wealthy parents, it may be that their wealth has enabled us to do things which are a part of this life's mission. If they are poor, it may be that we have lessons to learn about survival and hardship.

3. **We may see in a person's behavior in a single day manifestations of more than one past lifetime.** Just as I have come to see in Alex almost daily manifestations of each of several past lifetimes, so should we look at others in this way. A person is extremely complex. If we realize that in our 20's we may be joining part of our soul group to accomplish a group mission, it may be that sometime in our 30's we are to pursue and achieve another mission which reflects personality traits from yet another lifetime from the past. Becoming conscious of these complexities and learning to look for

them will expand our consciousness, and prepare us for our continuing journey of self-discovery.

4. **Analyze the things you are most interested in.** They are clues to your past lives. You choose the books you read, movies you see, places you visit or vacation for a reason. They may be familiar to you because you have been there in a past lifetime. They may help you in the mission you are on in this lifetime. Analyze your **choices** from the big ones to the little ones. Why did you choose one thing rather than another? There is a reason.

5. **Study your behavior or that of others when it doesn't fit in.** If a habit, interest or behavior doesn't fit the mold of your hometown, friends or family, which may be considered odd or unusual, it may be a clue. Study it to see if it would have been normal in another place or time. That may be where you lived in a previous lifetime. Once you get down to the time or place where it does fit in, study its history to see if there was a person who lived then and there with your profession or interests. Learn as much about him or her as you can. It may have been you in that lifetime.

4

No one could have stood up against him or stopped him except the gods, when he burst in the gates. HIS EYES FLASHED FIRE.

Among military leaders it would be difficult in history to find anyone whose charismatic leadership could match that of Alexander the Great.

Feeling as though I were now being led in my quest to uncover the spiritual lineage of Arthur Rimbaud, I was on a historical research adventure and expedition like nothing I had ever known. The concept that Arthur Rimbaud would have been Alexander the Great in a past lifetime and Yuya, Lt. General of the Charioteers and Officiate of the Temple of Min in Egypt nearly a thousand years before that, was charting a new course of possibilities. It could transform our understanding of the development of personality and of history itself. Make no mistake, I am saying here that the same spirit resided in these separate bodies successively, and into each new body, knowledge and remembrance of achievements and events of the past lives were buried in the recesses of their repressed memories. Some of them might have emerged negatively as phobic reactions (which Dr. Brian Weiss explores in *Many*

Lives, Many Masters), or positively as talents and abilities, which I am exploring here.

Most importantly, I was looking for personality traits from previous lifetimes, showing up in each new life. And more than that I was looking for a continuation of an individual mission which recurs and messages which are reinterpreted to each new generation by the bearer. When the spirit having lived in the body of Yuya came to dwell in the body of Alcibiades, he found himself deprived of a father at a very early age (four), and this left him in that lifetime devoid of many things an older man (father or father figure) teaches a younger one.

He had not learned restraint, modesty, or moderation. His brash and self centered behavior kept people constantly suspicious of him, and these traits prevented him from his goals as a leader and military commander. In studying Alexander, I came to realize that this spirit had succeeded in meeting these goals as Alexander, which he had not achieved as Alcibiades:

(1) Building on the successes of his father as a military man and expanding his father's vision by conquering Asia, (2) gaining from his father's acquiring for him the best tutors, including Aristotle, (3) adding to his male strength in competing with his father in male-male rivalry, and (4) surrounding himself with male military minded friends, some of whom were automatically in the company of his father, he had a base of psychological support—a virtual springboard to victory—that had eluded his spirit as Alcibiades.

The books I had read in my reading journey had proposed that in spirit form between lifetimes, we reassemble with our soul group—a joyous reunion of people we love who are not inhibited in spirit form by the complex feelings we have here in this lifetime. In that state between lifetimes, we choose our parents for the coming lifetime, based on their ability to put us in a position to achieve our next lifetime mission and purpose. This is coordinated with other members of our soul group who will appear in our next lifetime at strategic times and locations.

Had Alcibiades chosen parents for his next lifetime, he certainly chose two parents to match his ambitions. Alexander's father was Philip of Macedonia in the mountainous regions north of Athens. Starting with his marriage to Alexander's mother, the story sounds like pure Greek mythology—stories of the Greek gods and goddesses.

In rereading many of the accounts of Alexander's life, it is difficult for me as a writer not to want to share every sentence with the reader. Most of us have times in our lifetime where we are resting, or taking a break, or catching up, or simply doing mundane things for a while. But every phase of Alexander's life seemed full and explosive with meaning and action.

Alexander the Great was born in 356 B. C. Philip as a young man fell in love with Olympias, when he was in Samothrace, and married her there. According to Plutarch, the night before the wedding, she dreamed that a thunderbolt fell upon her body. It kindled a great fire. It produced divided flames which were dispersed all about. They were then extinguished. Philip, after he was married to Olympias, dreamed that he sealed up her body with a seal. The impression, he dreamed, was that of the figure of a lion.

Some said that Olympias was a sorceress, and once when Philip was preparing to go to bed with her found a serpent in the bed. It was said that this had destroyed the passion he felt for her (not surprisingly). In Samothrace, where Olympias was from, people were said to be extremely addicted to the enthusiastic Orphic rites, and the wild worship of Bacchus. Olympias not only had these mystical powers, she was extremely demanding, and strong willed, and exerted such control over both Philip and Alexander, that Alexander had trouble just being with her at times. It also shows that the Rites of Spring Festivals which Alex compulsively organized each year not only had its origins in Yuya, Officiate at the Temple of Min in Egypt, but in the Bacchinals he had watched his mother preside over and, in which he had taken part from earliest childhood, when he wold have been Alexander the Great. So strong was Olympias' power over her son Alexander, that some say he was afraid of her.

According to Plutarch, describing the Bacchic festivals she led, Olympias, to make them more fanatical and to more enthusiastically inspire the participants, would have great serpents wrapped around her. To add more barbaric dread, she would have serpents creeping out of the ivy in the mystic fans. She would have them wrapped around the sacred spears and in the women's garlands and necklaces for inspiration, so they would perform with more barbaric dread. Not surprisingly, the men would look upon all this with terror. Perhaps most important, Olympias was a proud molossian whose ancestry could be traced to Achilles, the hero of the Trojan War. This genetic connection was reinforced by Alexander's tutor Aristotle. He held Achilles up as a role model. This drew special attention from Alexander, who believed Achilles blood ran through his own veins. Alexander intended to live up to his ancestor's reputation, and he encouraged comparisons between himself and his legendary forebear.

Not unlike stories of the Greek gods, it was frequently pointed out that Alexander was born on the day the temple of Diana at Ephesus was burned. Hegesias of Magnesia said that the temple caught on fire and burned while its mistress was absent assisting with the birth of Alexander. All of the Eastern soothsayers, who happened to be at Ephesus, looked at the ruin of the temple as a forerunner to some other calamity. They ran around the town screaming that the day had brought forth something that would be fatal and destructive to all of Asia. (Perhaps there is a connection to my student Alex's being seized by an illness at Ephesus on a recent trip there and having to cut short his trip and return home early.)

It was customary in Ancient Greece at this time for young men to work out their bodies in a palestra or gymnasium (literally a place where exercise was done naked) between the ages of 13 and 18. They worked out six to eight hours a day in front of a statue of a perfect male body seeking perfection in developing each muscle group of their own. This was designed to give each young man enormous self-confidence. In a similar fashion the mind was exercised by tutors and scholars who between exercises lectured in the colonnade at the sides of the gymnasium's courtyard or beside the practice fields. In this setting, Alexander learned from his tutor Aristotle. Here he developed a life long friendship with Hephaestion, a fellow student his own age. It appeared to be clearly the deepest and most meaningful friendship of his life. So deep was his friendship with Hephaestion that when he died at 32, by the side of Alexander, Alexander was so furious he had the physician who attended him slain, and Alexander built a funeral pyre in the desert the height of a 20 story building.

Alexander was so well trained that when Philip went away to war, when Alexander was 16, he made Alexander regent of Macedonia. During this time there was an uprising, and 16–year-old Alexander simply took out the army and put down the uprising. In our present society, when I see efforts being made to extend boyhood into the mid-twenties, I point out that in Classical Greece a male was considered a man at 13. Even in Colonial America, at 14 young men were schooled and ready to run the plantations inherited from their fathers. I am fond of saying, "Alexander was a man and conquered his first country at 16." Philip II had become king of Macedonia in 359 when Alexander was three. Philip was murdered in 336 and Alexander became King Alexander III. Thus Alexander became King at 20. He proceeded to conquer Persia (a dream of his father's), then to India. There his troops grew weary, and he returned to Persia where Hephaestion died in 324, and Alexander died on June 13, 323 B. C. at the age of 32.

Various reasons such as malaria or typhoid fever are given by some scholars explaining the deaths of Hephaestion and Alexander. But in the biography *Alexander the Great, The Invisible Enemy* by John Maxwell O'Brien, he points to excessive partying and heavy drinking on the part of Alexander and the whole company of soldiers who surrounded him, particularly their indulgence in wine. Alexander had had from his earliest teen years in school a loyal group of friends who were referred to as the Royal Companions and the Royal Bodyguards. They were devoted to Alexander. But they also followed him into revelry before and after their conquests.

When I first began discussing these past lives with the contemporary Alex, it was difficult for me to tell whether Alex accepted the possibility that he could be in the spiritual lineage of such greats as Rimbaud, and

Alcibiades. He, nor I, had ever heard of Yuya, but that past life seemed to fall in line with the others. Alex would patiently listen, and when I would ask a question, he would tell me whether or not it had meaning or was applicable to his life.

I would ask him a leading question, thinking that if my supposition were correct, he would corroborate it by answering in a certain way. In New York, I had asked if he had ever heard of Arthur Rimbaud, thinking that if I were on the right track he would say yes. Not only did he say yes, but he had told me that he had formed a poetry reading at the art school in New York shortly after he arrived, and that he had chosen to read Rimbaud's famous poem, "The Drunken Boat." This was like hitting the jackpot, the ideal answer, if I were on the right track.

But as I continued my research and began to read more about Alcibiades and Alexander, leading their troops into battle, I began to share more about what I was coming to believe was his spiritual lineage. Then, Alex began to share stories that he thought might be relevant. For nearly three years we met once a week in Atlanta for dinner and had discussions which usually went from three to eight hours.

During one such dinner, almost as an aside, he shared an episode in his life that occurred when he was 16 and living with his family in a small town in Iowa. It seems that he and a half dozen boys, who were his closest friends—all 16—had been arrested one night at 3 a.m. "What in the world for?" I asked. He explained that he had been leading his companions on a charge down a quiet residential street screaming and yelling at the tops of their voices—all stark naked. Obviously this woke up the neighbors, and they called the police.

Instantly I recognized this as a reenactment of an historical event in a previous lifetime of Alex. "You were Alexander, at 16 leading your troops into battle," I exclaimed. At the time of Alcibiades and Alexander, young men charged into battles naked, except for having a shield and wearing a helmet to protect them from the enemy's swords and, of course, carrying a sword themselves. Sometimes they may have had a chlamys (which was all most young men wore most of the time in classical Greece). A chlamys was a single garment about the size of a towel, thrown over one shoulder, perhaps to keep from getting their shoulders blistered in the hot Mediterranean sun. (This was before the spread into the region of Near Eastern religions, which had taken hold in climates where life was hard. They taught that one should feel shame or guilt for showing one's naked body. In Classical Greece, where everyone trained endlessly to make of their bodies something beautiful, one's body was seen as a gift from the gods, to be proud of and honored, not to be hidden or covered up, or about which to feel ashamed. They did not see anything wrong with the human body, which they saw as being beautiful and a creation and gift of the gods. It was displayed openly at the Olympic games, where all the participants competed naked, and the Olympics games were a religious event.)

Not only was Alex that night in Iowa when he was 16 running naked (as he had done as Alcibiades and Alexander in foot races and athletic events), but he may have been reliving and remembering one of Alexander's first military battles. I could not wait until I got home to look it up.

When Philip was away on an expedition against the Byzantines, he had left Alexander, then 16, his lieutenant in Macedonia. He had committed his charge and seal to him. While his father was away, Alexander took out the army and reduced the rebelling Maedi. Alexander took their chief towns by storm. He drove out the barbarous inhabitants, and replaced them with inhabitants of several nations in their place. To top it all he called the place after his own name, "Alexandropolis." Later at the battle of Chaeronea, where his father fought the Grecians, he was said to have been the first man to charge the Thebans "sacred band."

Alex's story of his naked charge down a quiet Iowa neighborhood, seems unexplainable, since I have never heard of a such behavior before, unless we see it as a kind of instinctive reenactment of something he had done before, buried in his subconscious memory. It added an insight to my growing awareness of past lives: We relive things we have done in past lives because we (subconsciously) remember them. We are repeating things we have done in a past life at approximately the same age we did it before, perhaps because it was so dramatic and so filled with meaning for us. So we are constantly reliving things we have done in past lives, without realizing it.

As our weekly dinner discussions continued, Alex and I both began to see his previous lifetimes as something to take for granted. As he moved into his mid-twenties, his passion for his annual Rites of Spring became more intense. More specifically, his passion for partying became more intense. While this was a characteristic of his generation, it began to concern him and me that it was becoming dangerous to his health. When one works 40 hours a week and stays up partying until dawn three or four nights a week, it becomes a health hazard. Alex was working up to five days and nights—working 8–hour days and partying all night—without sleep. As he began to approach 30, he began to show signs of the physical damage he was doing to his body. Such behavior was straight out of Alexander's march through Persia, a lifestyle Alexander was exhibiting when he was the same age as Alex:

On one of his expeditions, when Alexander the Great marched into Gedrosia, he continued his march through Carmania. He was feasting all the way for seven days. He had with him his most intimate friends. They banqueted and reveled night and day upon a platform, which they erected on a lofty scaffold. The scaffold was drawn slowly by eight horses as they partied. This was followed by a long row of chariots, where his commanders and friends were constantly supplied with fresh food and drink. They had garlands around their heads like crowns.

In this procession music was supplied with pipes and flutes. It was all compared to the rites of Bacchus. It was a bacchanal. Long before my research on this spiritual lineage began, Alex described his parties himself as "bacchanals" with his making many references to Bacchus.

As Alex's addiction to partying went beyond his Rites of Springs, we began to discuss seriously, many times, how he might curtail his revelry so that it did not damage his health and shorten his life. The theme of our discussions was, "Perhaps what he was to learn in this lifetime, was how to live beyond 32—longer than he lived as Alexander."

So frequent were our comparisons, that once after Alex had a very strong willed woman move in to live with him, he was having an extremely difficult time maintaining his independence. On successfully reestablishing his independent occupation of his own apartment after insisting she move out, we met for dinner. When he came in, his eyes were wild. He exclaimed, "SHE IS OLYMPIAS!"

A recurring characteristic and interest of Alex had been what he described, after returning from a visit with a friend in Wisconsin, as "Nude Power." He claimed he had discovered the "power" one feels of being naked. He had made the discovery at a session of "skinny dipping" when he and a group of friends had gone swimming in a river late one night. He encouraged his fellow male friends to exercise their rights to shed their clothes. No doubt the girls screamed in shock, when their dates reemerged from around the bend of the river with nothing on. These 'Nude Power" happenings became a regular feature of Alex's ventures away from Atlanta, when he would be visiting at someone's cabin or mountain retreat.

Here again, no one I knew at the time exhibited such interests or behavior. Was this too, something from the past? Alex had been a student at the farm, which I later learned had an incredible Native American history. After searching through the history I had concluded that also in Alex's spiritual lineage was John Ridge, son of Major Ridge, a leader of the Cherokee Nation. Alex's family (after living in Wisconsin and Iowa) had returned to Georgia, and the site of their apartment was but a short distance, perhaps five miles, from New Echota, the capital of the Cherokee Nation. After graduation from the art school in New York, Alex returned to live for a year with his parents and get a job to save money to start paying off his student loans. He got a job at an outlet mall. All this was happening while I was doing research on this Cherokee family.

To my amazement some pieces of the historical puzzle fell into place that year. A house, reported to be the home of John Ridge, was just a mile south of the outlet mall where Alex was working. The road he had to take to get to work would have been the same road John Ridge also took daily going from his home to work and meetings at New Echota.

Looking for the same personality traits in John Ridge that I had seen in Alex, I found accounts that, as a youth, John Ridge loved to go naked. He would be seen, well approaching adulthood, walking naked, wading and kicking water in the streams of Oothcalooga Creek, near where his father lived. He loved to shock the puritanical and prudish white European settlers in the area who would come to the creek and find this young Cherokee prince proudly prancing through the water without a stitch of clothing. In reading a diary of a Moravian Missionary who taught at a missionary school in Chattanooga, Tennessee near Chickamauga Creek, I read that the missionary had visited the school to give a guest lecture.

He was impressed by the well behaved little Indian boys and girls, sitting politely with hands folded neatly on their desks. Then he records how that all changed, as soon as the bell rang for recess. The children went out of the building whooping and hollering, and ran straight for the creek, which flowed near the school. One boy led the others, he recorded, in taking off all his clothes, leading all the others to do the same—boys and girls—following him until they had all jumped into the creek stark naked laughing and frolicking.

The visiting missionary at the Chattanooga mission was horrified, as his diary describes in great detail, and he lectured the headmaster on bringing order to these "savages." Not at that first reading, but later I read, that the brightest student there at that time, and the leader among the students, was none other than—John Ridge. No doubt this joy that John Ridge found in shocking people with his nude stunts had been preserved and celebrated once again in his new life as Alex. If we extend the behavior back to Alcibiades and Alexander, we would realize that he was only doing what was natural for all normal and healthy young men in those times.

John Ridge went on to become a leader of his people. His father Major Ridge, and his two first cousins—Elias Boudinot and Stand Watie formed what was known as "The Treaty Party." For years they urged the American government in Washington to recognize that the Cherokees were the rightful owners of their lands—virtually all of northwest Georgia—between what is now Atlanta and Chattanooga. The Cherokee government in Council at New Echota had decided to take their cause to the U. S. Supreme Court. They did and the Supreme Court ruled in their favor. But Andrew Jackson, who was president at the time, refused to enforce the Court's ruling. Once they saw that their cause was hopeless, and seeking to prevent death and destruction of their people, The Treaty Party (the Ridge-Watie family) urged a peaceful settlement and removal west. Consequently they signed a treaty, but it did not represent a majority of the Cherokee people whose representatives did not attend the meeting. A rival chief, John Ross, had urged the Cherokees to stay.

History proved The Treaty Party right, because those who didn't agree and move west, were forcibly removed by the U. S. Army in 1838, known as the "Trail of Tears." It resulted in the deaths of 4,000 people, whose lives would have been spared had they heeded the advice of the Ridge-Watie leadership. When the remainder of the Cherokees arrived in Oklahoma at the end of the forced march, they found that the Ridge-Watie leadership had set up a government that had been in place over a year. Assassination parties were sent out, and John Ridge (like his father and cousin Elias Boudinot) was assassinated. One of the similarities here was that the death of John Ridge was like that of Alcibiades—both by assassination.

Adding John Ridge to the lineage of Yuya, Alcibiades, Alexander the Great and Arthur Rimbaud was also focusing attention on spiritual lineages in each of their soul groups, and I will discuss this in a future chapter. What researching John Ridge at this time was doing, was explaining the behavior of Alex, who was doing nothing more in present day than exhibiting behavior he had shown as Alcibiades, Alexander and John Ridge.

John Ridge became one of the most eloquent spokesman for the cause of the Cherokee people, and his speeches are quoted to this day—perhaps eloquence learned in speeches he had made as Alcibiades and Alexander and in poetry he had written as Arthur Rimbaud. Rimbaud died just a decade before John Ridge was born.

LESSONS LEARNED—CHAPTER FOUR

1. **Everyone should recognize that he or she is here with a mission.** If it takes a lifetime to figure out what that is, take the lifetime. Better to figure out your purpose late in life, than live out your life without ever knowing why. A distant cousin who had lived for a year in the Northeast returned to Georgia, where in his small town, he observed that no one questioned anything. They simply did what was expected of them—expected by their parents, family, teachers, school, peers, and people in their hometown. He compared them to "drunken pigs bouncing off of walls." While I thought this analogy was rather severe, it makes a point. The point is how wasteful it is to be given the gift of a lifetime without asking the most important questions a person can ask: "Who am I?" "Why am I here?" "What is my purpose in life." "How can I make life better for those around me and those who will follow?"

2. **Develop a role model.** Alexander's role model was Achilles. Who in history, or who do you know, has lived a life you would model you own after? We are not free floating in space, unless we have no goals or models to pursue. One of the striking lessons of both Alcibiades and Alexander is that we need not look beyond man-kind's own history to find heroes. In filtering through all the mind-less jungle of uninteresting stories that fill our movie screens and television sets, I wondered as I read about these two men, "Here are role models for any age."

3. **Energy is a key.** We see in Alcibiades and Alexander, and later in Rimbaud, incredible energy, bursting at the seams—exploding in gallant and daring behavior. They are not afraid of anything, and they fly through danger enduring all to accomplish their missions. They should serve as inspirations to all of us. Rimbaud's colossal energy has inspired writers and artists ever since. It was the guiding inspiration to the entire Surrealist movement which included his own future life as Andre Breton, spokesman for the movement,

which included Picasso, Dali, Braque and others. Seeing Rimbaud's wide travels before settling in Africa as veiled "remembering" and unconscious "retracing" of Alexander's travels and military campaigns provides a whole new understanding of Rimbaud's life. His searching for a male friend comparable to Hephaestion gives us a sad insight into his lonely life as a poet seemingly stranded in time.

5

And being, as Plato would have, the scholar-like and philosophical temper.

Just as I began to think about a possible subsequent lifetime in Rome, as if by arrangement, the film *Gladiator* appeared on television. As I again watched the scenes of ancient Rome recreated on film for the audience, I found myself thinking, "My Rome." How many times in a previous lifetime, I approached the city from a distance as shown in the artistic rendering in this film, and felt relief that I was coming "home."

My first affinity with Rome occurred in the fifth grade. I would have been 11 years old, and I chose for a class project the Roman Senate. I did a term paper complete with drawings of the Roman Senate, including clothing the senators would have worn. I remember particularly drawing the kind of curve on the seats in which the senators would have been seated. I drew the kinds of homes people in Rome would have lived in. At that time there was a flood of movies about ancient Rome, and I saw them every one. I have come to believe that our selectively in having favorite historical periods and locations in movies we choose to see and books we choose to read, is the result of our having lived there or then in that place or time in history. It is the familiarity with the time and place—our experienced and repressed memories of having been there, which draw us—pull us—to relive that time from our past in current books, television programs, films or plays at the theatre.

In addition I made A's in all courses related to ancient Greece or ancient Rome. I had slowly, almost unconsciously, begun accumulating a collection of books that included reconstructed models of Rome—the Forum, Palatine Hill, and the Circus Maximus. I kept, until they were ragged, old issues of the National Geographic Magazines, complete with text and drawings of the reconstructed eras of ancient Greece and ancient Rome.

It was at the conclusion of my first year at Yale, when I managed to get to Europe. It was my own carefully planned "grand tour"—13 countries in 13 weeks, visiting every major museum, cathedral and castle in each country. When I got to Rome I could hardly wait to get to the ruins of the Roman Forum. Here was where the Roman Senate met (the subject of my drawings of when I was 11). I discovered Palatine Hill, which towered over the forum, and on the other side of it was the Circus Maximus. At the end of the Forum rose the ruins of the Coliseum.

I arrived at the Forum a little after noon, following an early lunch. I began walking through the ruins of the buildings of the forum, then up and around to the top of Palatine Hill, then to the other side to look down on the ruins of the Circus Maximus, famed for its chariot races. For those who have been there, you may remember that we are not talking about a great deal of space and distance. I wandered and walked over these "familiar" streets, passages, vistas, slopes, hilltops, over and over and over. Almost before I knew it, the skies were getting dark. I had been there for eight hours! Walking over and over each location—looking up and down each street, feeling over and over again, the way each location felt. As darkness approached, I could not believe that I had spent the entire afternoon, wandering these familiar streets and passages. And as darkness descended, I could hardly tear myself away. I did not want to leave, even then, but when I could no longer see my way, and needing to find a place that served dinner, I finally departed.

What had drawn me with such incredible strength and passion to this location? What had led me at the early age of 11 to capture in word and image, Roman senators standing to speak in the Roman Forum in ancient Rome? Whatever it was, it seemingly that day that it would not turn loose of me, as I wandered those streets *again*. If I had lived either as Plato or someone close to him in a previous lifetime, then would there have been someone in ancient Rome, who would have been a kind of logical successor to him? Would there have been someone whose life and background would enable Plato in a next lifetime, to achieve some of his ongoing goals?

I began to study historical figures in ancient Rome. I took an encyclopedia of personalities in this period of history, and beginning with the writers and poets, began systematically developing a theoretical scenario of whose life would have best succeeded Plato's, and whose personality traits or talents might be evidenced in my life in some way.

After exhausting one possibility after another, I eventually focused on Plato's belief in a benevolent dictator, which he put forward in his dialogue *The Republic*. Of the persons I studied in Rome, there would have been a perfect successor to Plato—someone, who in fact put into practice Plato's concept of the benevolent dictator himself: Marcus Tullius Cicero. Cicero would have put Plato's theory into practice when he served as a Consul of the Roman Empire. Furthermore, Cicero's role as a statesman in the Roman Senate, reinforced some of Plato's ideals without compromise. In fact, it was Cicero's refusal to compromise which put his life in danger.

Cicero was plagued with some personality problems. He fought his lack of modesty and tendency to objectively describe and talk about his considerable talents and abilities as a public speaker. Anytime someone is truthful about his talents and abilities, especially if they are considerable, it is a very unpopular thing to do. Even truthful statements may be considered a show of conceit or arrogance. Modesty Cicero did not have.

In addition, he had a domineering hen-pecking wife, who attempted to drive him to meet her expectations in his political and professional accomplishments. This led him to push himself in a way that may not have seemed natural and may have been an irritant to others. Nonetheless, during the time he was consul, he was able to put Plato's theories into practice, and demonstrated what many of Plato's dialogues of Socrates' teachings advocated: living a good life.

Once I began to focus my attention on Cicero, I was not at all surprised to find that he had lived on the side of Palatine Hill. The streets and byways which I found myself walking over time and again that afternoon in Rome were the very same streets that Cicero walked daily from his home to and from the Senate and to other affairs of state.

Cicero was born in 106 B. C. and died in 43 B. C. He was a member of the Senate at the time of Julius Caesar's assassination, though he was not present at the time nor a part of the conspiracy against Caesar.

My early search for similarities in the life of Plato and Cicero were quickly rewarded. Cicero was quaestor in Sicily. On two occasions Plato had spent time in Sicily as well as Syracuse. Early records suggest that Cicero was a prodigy. According to Plutarch, at an early age in his lessons he became known for his quickness in learning. His reputation grew among the boys in his class, and Cicero's father would visit the school to witness his son's brilliance first hand.

Even Plutarch saw the similarity I was searching for. When the similarity I'm looking for presents itself in such overwhelming evidence and with such clarity, it is difficult for me not to believe that I was being "led." By now, many times, I had thought of the teaching of Jesus, when he said, "Ask, and it will be given you; seek and you shall find; knock and it will be opened unto you. For everyone who asks receives, and he who seeks finds, and to him who knocks it will be opened." (Matthew 7:7–8) I wondered if this applied not only to the seeking which I was doing, but the research all historians and scientists undertake when they seek to expand mankind's knowledge of the universe and the world we live in. Clearly, my theories and projections were being proven right with such regularly, I had to consider this possibility.

Even Plutarch described Plato as having a scholar-like and philosophical temper. Cicero was praised for being eager in every kind of learning, and open to all kinds of knowledge and instruction. He was considered at the same time the best orator and the best poet in Rome. No wonder he had an ego problem.

When Cicero took up the defense of an unpopular cause, he was fearful of gaining the wrath of Sylla, who had led troops in the Marsian war. So he left for Athens, where he adhered to the doctrines of what was then called the New Academy—thus, he followed a pattern I was now looking for—that we are often unconsciously and unknowingly walking over our faded footprints from past lives. Here the "reincarnated" Plato, had returned not only to his old home Athens, but to the very Academy which he had led.

Cicero did military service under Pompius Strabo (the father of Pompey), and much of his public life revolved around his support of Pompey in public affairs. His first important political speech was against the political conservatives in the senate, and was in favor of conferring on Pompey command of a campaign against Mithradates, king of Pontus. But it was later with the support of this conservative element (Optimates), who feared the revolutionary ideas of his rival, Cataline, that Cicero was elected consul in 63 B.C. So intense was his rivalry with Cataline that when he presided over the consular elections in 63 B. C., Cicero wore armor beneath his toga. Cataline lost, and he planned to lead an armed uprising in Italy and start fires in Rome. So grave was the danger, that Cicero had trouble convincing the senate of the degree of the danger.

He finally persuaded the senators to pass the equivalent of martial law on October 22. After escaping an attempt on his life, Cicero spoke against Cataline in the senate. That night Cataline fled Rome, but evidence was gathered against the conspirators. Cato spoke for execution, and Caesar was against it. But since Cicero was responsible, the execution took place.

Cicero announced the death of the conspirators with a single word: "vixerunt" ("they are dead"). This received a tremendous ovation from everyone. Cicero was thus inspired to an appeal in politics to "concordia ordinum," "concord between the classes." At this high point in his life, Catalus declared Cicero "father of his country."

At the end of 60 B. C., Julius Caesar invited Cicero to join a political alliance he was forming with Crassus and Pompey. At this point we see Cicero, at the height of his popularity and power, making a hard decision between practicality and ideal. The handwriting on the wall said, these are the powerful leaders of the country. It is to your self-interest to join them. You can further gain a foothold for your ideals in this alliance.

Instead, Cicero was true to his ideals. He considered it unconstitutional. Julius Caesar again made an effort to include him, offering him a place on his staff in Gaul in 59 B. C. A year later Publius Clodius became tribune. Cicero had antagonized Clodius by giving evidence against him in 61, when he was tried for profanity. Cicero, sensing now that he was in danger, fled Rome.

Cicero went first to Thessalonica, in Macedonia, and then to Illyricum. Cicero had been declared an exile in a bill Clodius had had passed. But in 57 B. C., efforts by Pompey and the tribune Milo had him recalled to Rome. Cicero landed at Brundisium (modern day Brindisi). He was hailed along the route of his return, and arrived in Rome a month later.

In 57–56 B. C., Cicero tried to estrange Pompey from Caesar, but this failed. Instead Pompey persuaded Cicero to align himself with the three (Pompey, Caesar and Crassus), and he did. He committed himself in writing and delivered a speech, the "palinode" affirming this. He felt compelled to make a number of defenses in public life he found disagreeable, and so he abandoned public life for a while and wrote "De oratore" and "De republica" and began "De legibus." In 51 B. C., he was persuaded to leave Rome and to govern the province of Cilicia, which is in Asia Minor, for a year. For this he was praised as governing with integrity.

In my ongoing research to discover strong impulses, attractions to ancient places or times, one of my strongest is the Altar at Pergamon. Pergamon is located in Asia Minor near the Aegean Coast between ruins of ancient Troy and Ephesus. Pergamon itself is now an ancient ruin—it had an acropolis (hilltop of public and sacred buildings and temples like the acropolis in Athens). The Altar at Pergamon has always been one of the most beautiful architectural structures I have ever seen. I would pour over its picture in the Encyclopedia Britannica, when I was young—from seven up, along with those of the Acropolis in Athens. I would draw blueprints of the Great Altar at Pergamon, draw sketches of it, and, like my dreams for an Athenian Acropolis in Dalton on Mount Rachel, I would imagine a Great Altar of Pergamon being built somewhere in north Georgia. It was an object of fascination and love.

In the spring of 2000, I told a friend about this fascination prior to a trip to Europe. By now, I was convinced that I must have lived in Pergamon in a previous lifetime, and it was my repressed memories from that lifetime which attracted me. My friend insisted that I go to the Pergamon Museum in Berlin. Every time I spoke to her, she would bring it up. Even after I got to Europe, she e-mailed me to remind me about going. Her insistence was so unusual, it had come to fit my description of something out of the ordinary, which we should assume was a guiding hand in our research. Using Dr. Brian Weiss' term, "Master Spirits," I would say that her insistence was not hers. She had become an instrument of the Master Spirits directing me there. In Berlin, when I checked into my hotel I learned that my travel agent unknowingly had put me in a hotel only a few blocks from the Pergamon Museum.

Needless to say, the visit to the museum was a religious experience. Much of the original altar had been moved from Turkey to Berlin and reassembled. Elsewhere in the museum, was the statue of Athena that had been in the library on the Pergamon acropolis adjacent to the Altar. I had left the museum, before I realized I had not seen the statue of Athena. I had earlier learned that Athena, the patron goddess of Athens and also the goddess of wisdom, was the patron goddess of Plato, and also of Cicero! At this point, I had concluded that she must be mine as well, and I had not very subtly placed a picture of her statue—complete with shield and helmet in my apartment.

On a different day I found my way to the statue of Athena at the Gropius Museum, where the statue of Athena had been moved. Finding my way to the appropriate gallery on the second floor, I approached the statue slowly and from a side room. There were many glass cases, exhibiting smaller items in the room. I first saw the statue of Athena through these glass cases, and the image was reflected through them almost like a piece of modern sculpture.

Inexplicably, I was breathing hard as I slowly inched my way past the glass cases, with each step the statue coming more clearly into view. Once my view was clear as I passed the last case, it took my breath away. I felt a great impulse to bow, as I might have done in ancient times, to show my respect and appreciation for her guidance in this and my past lives.

As I moved to the right, I realized the statue had been placed to be at the end of a long corridor, with other art objects along its side. Down that corridor was a guard and other tourists. I moved back to the side, and there compulsively, and discreetly out of view of the guards and other tourists, I knelt to floor, pressing my forehead to it, and offered my prayers of thanksgiving to this goddess to whom all of Athens had looked for guidance. Perhaps I was now repeating, reliving, an act of respect I had done many times before at Pergamon and at the Parthenon in Athens.

I learned from the incredible virtual reality display on the side wall that this statue is the oldest statue of Athena in existence. The original statue in the Parthenon in the Acropolis in Athens had been made of perishable materials, but this one, carved at the time, when the original was still in place in Athens, had been made as a duplicate. The expression on Athena's face was extraordinary—peaceful and calm. One did not want to stop looking at her.

The virtual reality animated movie gave the view one might have had from a helicopter landing on the ancient Pergamon acropolis. Just up from the altar was the library, and it was the library that left me spellbound. The animated film showed the view one would have had walking toward the library. Then the two giant wooden doors creaked open with a loud noise. One would have entered it with respect and awe as one would enter a cathedral. It must have felt like a cathedral of learning, because upon entering, after passing through those giant wooden doors, there would have been a spectacular view at the end of this massive lobby of this very statue of Athena. How appropriate I thought, that one would enter a library with reverence facing a towering statue of a goddess—because Athena was the goddess of wisdom! Who else to be the center piece of a library? To the side were large wooden cabinet doors, and inside them were scrolls—the books and the stacks of their day. Then the camera took us through a large door to the left to a porch overlooking the open market place area below. Even animated curtains were blowing in the breeze. It was so effective I could easily imagine the sounds of crowds in the marketplace and people moving about in the city. Again, I did not want to leave. I watched this entire animated recreation at least a half dozen times, while other tourists would pause and watch it with me.

I had said, well into my reading journey, that libraries are like churches. Libraries are religious institutions. They are repositories of knowledge. Dr. Brian Weiss said in *Many Lives, Many Masters* that our goal is to grow in knowledge and love. I had concluded two years into this journey, that increase of knowledge *automatically* produces increase of love. The builders of this library at Pergamon understood this. What better way to enter a building to begin doing your research than entering it face to face with a goddess? When I was at Yale, I would always choose to study at the main undergraduate library. The entrance is built like an abbey or cathedral. Where the altar might have been was a Guttenburg Bible, lighted under a glass case, all very appropriate I thought.

I had originally thought that Plato might have spent a while studying at the library at Pergamon, or perhaps beginning the writing of his dialogues here. But the problem is that the altar and other public buildings were not in existence that early. They would have been built by the time of Cicero, and I was thinking it may have been that Cicero who may have visited Pergamon going to or from Cilicia, which is farther south and east in Asia Minor (now Turkey). Still, I could not find a record of Cicero visiting or writing anything here. In 2001, I wrote, "In my personal experience, though, there is little doubt that my association with this place in a past life was real and powerful. If not with Plato or Cicero, it may have been later. Whoever or whenever, it would have been a perfect place to write. And my search for its significance will continue."

The following year, I discovered that it *was* a later time, and it would have been Galen, a physican and writer for whom I was searching. Galen was born in 130 and died in 200. It was he who would have been born in Pergamon. He was born the son of a well respected architect. His plan was to study philosophy, but his father had a dream that he should become a physician. The Asclepion, the medical school of those times, would have been halfway between his home and the Pergamon acropolis. No doubt while walking to the Pergamon library on the acropolis, he would have walked past and greatly admired the Great Altar at Pergamon. He would have been on his way to study at the very library that had moved me so in Berlin. Like Cicero, he was "known for his lectures and writings," he wrote 500 treatises on medicine and philosophy. He could have been a character in the movie *Gladiator,* since he started his medical career as a physician to gladiators in Pergamon, like the one in the outlying province depicted in the movie. Then Galen went to Rome, where he became court physician to three emperors including all of those depicted in the film, including Marcus Aurelius and Comodus. I consider this lifetime to have had a profound effect in my spiritual lineage, since I have in this lifetime an unusually large number of architects and doctors among my closest friends. I joke with my doctor friends by showing them pictures of the ruins of the Asclepion at Pergamon and saying, "This is where we studied together. This is where we were classmates."

When Cicero returned to Rome from Cilicia in 49 B.C., his friend Pompey and Caesar were in a power struggle. Cicero was on the outskirts of Rome when Caesar crossed the Rubicon and invaded Italy.

When Pompey was forced to leave Rome, Cicero chose to stay, and tried to state his own terms to Caesar. He realized, though, with each victory by Caesar, his own position was growing weaker.

In researching Cicero's behavior at this point, I came to realize that in most accounts of Julius Caesar's assassination, Caesar comes off the victim, and Brutus, Cassius and others are viewed as villains. What is rarely depicted is that Caesar was, in fact, becoming a dictator and destroying democracy in Rome. While one cannot agree with the means of the senators who were trying to save democracy in Rome, the legitimacy of their cause and honesty of their concern often seems to get lost—for example in Marc Antony's speech in Shakespeare's play.

Cicero was not involved in the conspiracy to murder Caesar nor in the act itself. He was absent from the senate when it happened. Later, he did speak in favor of a general amnesty. At this point he returned to his philosophical writings, and visited his son, who was studying in Athens (again walking on the faded footprints of Plato).

From Athens Cicero returned to Rome and reentered politics with a vengeance. He sought to use Julius Caesar's adopted son Octavian, but seriously underestimated Octavian's intelligence. He tried to persuade the senate to go after Antony. And he made an unfortunate remark about the youthful Octavian. He said that the young man should be given praise and distinctions—and then be disposed of. When this got back to Octavian, it led him to solidify a triumvirate of Octovian, Antony and Lepidus, excluding Cicero. Cicero had alienated Octavian *and* Antony. He had written against Antony in his *Phillipics.*

Octavian, once he had used Cicero to get himself elected counsel, essentially said farewell to Cicero. He reconciled himself to Antony and Lepidus, joining his power with theirs and divided the government with them, as though it were a piece of property, according to Plutarch. Once united, they made out a list of 200 persons to be put to death. The one causing the greatest debate was Cicero. Octavian wanted to spare Cicero, but Antony and Lepidus insisted on his death. On the third day of the debate Octavian gave in and agreed that he should be killed. When the soldiers finally came to seize him, a youth, who had been educated by Cicero in the liberal arts and sciences, an emancipated slave of his brother Quintus, Philologus, by name, told the soldiers where to find Cicero, who had fled to the seacoast. Cicero was on a litter on his way to the sea through an area where there were shady walks.

Herennius, the arresting tribune ran to the place where the walk came out from the shade trees. Emerging from the grove, and seeing the situation, Cicero commanded his servants to put his litter down. He stroked his chin with his left hand, as he was accustomed to doing. He looked directly at his murderers. Covered with dust, his beard and hair untrimmed, his sixty-four year old face showed his worries and stress. His friends and supporters turned their heads so they could not see what was coming. Cicero then stretched forth his head, his neck extended from the litter. Herennius then committed the murder by cutting off his head, and by Antony's command, also cutting off his hands by which he had written his Phillipics, styled orations against Antony. His head and hands were taken to Rome, where Antony was holding assembly, and he commanded Cicero's head and hands be fastened up on the rostrum, where the orators spoke. Plutarch recorded how the Romans shuddered at the sight, believing they not only were seeing the face of Cicero but the very image of Antony's own soul.

The story was told how years later, Octavian, now Caesar Augustus, had found the son of his daughter, reading one of Cicero's books. His grandson hid it under his gown, for fear that Caesar would be mad. Instead, his grandfather took the book from him, and after looking through a great part it, gave it back to his grandson and told him that this was written by a learned man and a lover of his country.

Of all his talents, Cicero, was known best for his skills in oratory. I reviewed any similarities I might have had. Looking at my own experience, for this trait to come down, I early excelled in public speaking, winning the "Merzick Prize" for excellence in Public Speaking at Yale. Much later, I was asked to teach Public Speaking at a college in North Georgia. I found myself thriving in this assignment, explaining the concept of "rhetoric" to my students, giving the history of its teaching in ancient Rome and ancient Greece. I used the description of Socrates of what speeches should contain from Plato's dialogue *Phaedrus*.

I copied on the board the prerequisites for a good speech directly from Plato. For example, Socrates had said of rhetorical art, that it was a way of directing the soul by means of speech. I thought, "Perhaps this was a view I had heard from the originator of it years before in a previous lifetime in Greece, and that is why I have chosen to use it in my teaching of public speaking."

The innovations I used in teaching these speech classes, I found also evident in some of Cicero's speeches. Recently, while I was in Baltimore, I attended a service at a church, where I had served on the staff many years before. To my amazement some of the members came up to me and quoted from a sermon I had delivered there more than 20 years before, and they said members of the congregation would discuss those points I had made from time to time over the years.

The degree to which, I have found public speaking exciting and enjoyable was evident in the mid 1990's. I was to deliver a speech at a statewide meeting of a Garden Association—in connection with the gardens at the historic farm, where I was conducting the arts program at that time. I thrived on any opportunity to promote the program I was directing.

Nearly a thousand people were present, and the span of my audience stretched 180 degrees in front of me. Just before I spoke, the chairman asked about 200 of the members to begin lining up to the right of the auditorium and proceed to a banquet table beside the raised speaker's platform. This means my challenge in keeping the attention and eye contact of the audience was enormous. Not only was I to continually span the 180 degree of seating directly in front of me, but I was also challenged to keep the attention of the people lining up on one side—keeping their attention as well as those distracted by the commotion.

I remember relishing this challenge and fought vigorously to keep the attention of every person in the hall. My goal was not to lose eye contact with a single person. I sought to hold everyone's gaze steadily while slowly moving my head from one side to the other, and especially focusing on those standing in the line. I was surprised and conscious myself of the extent of my pleasure in this challenge. It is the kind of challenge Cicero would have welcomed and enjoyed.

I have also been very conscious, throughout this lifetime, of the abundance of public speaking talent I have, which is not being used. This lifetime for me has not been one where I have chosen one profession and followed it throughout a whole lifetime. Had I chosen a lifetime in the ministry, where I could have been preaching every Sunday, or a lifetime in politics where I would have been making public speeches on a regular basis, this talent could have been better employed. This is a lesson for all of us. In each lifetime, we may have to be selective with our talents and abilities and only use those necessary for our mission. Again, it points toward the *importance* of the mission.

But the strongest and clearest mission I had in this lifetime was without doubt focused on the time I spent on that isolated farm in northwest Georgia. I spent 15 years in educational preparation for it, and more than 20 years doing it. Friends have reassured me that there is no way to measure the value of what those programs did for young people. My friends call it "the seeds that you planted," in making the lives better for so many people.

Now I am involved in an unanticipated Phase III of my life, which involves the writing of this book and efforts to film Plato's dialogues. Perhaps in these endeavors there will be more opportunities to use the public speaking abilities, which I seem to have inherited (or perhaps "remembered") from Cicero by being in his spiritual lineage or someone close to him.

From the study of Cicero, too, I have learned that our lives, in this lifetime, are successions of recollections, missions—large extended ones as well as mini-missions. We don't just walk over faded footprints from one lifetime, but from many. We don't just have one mission in a lifetime but several. Our individual missions may or may not be a part of a larger one.

Many of your personality traits, passions for places or activities, may have their origins and explanation in a past life you have lived. That is why seeking to discover and be educated in your own past lives is so important. It is the key to understanding who you, where you are going, and what you are here for.

I lament, when I see people, letting their time run out in this lifetime, like sand in the hourglass. Life consists of more than just having a 9–5 job, living a standard domestic life with a spouse and 2.3 children. This is why I complain occasionally to someone, when I see them wasting time or living their life the way someone else wants them to. When I see someone living just to serve another person's needs or ambitions, I complain that they look like they are just going to "pass" on this lifetime.

This book is intended to sound the alarm. Wake up and know that you are here for a reason, a purpose—unique in all the history of the world! Stand on your own two feet, and see where you have been (in past lives) and where you are going.

LESSONS LEARNED—CHAPTER FIVE

1. **Your talents and abilities have a history in a past lifetime.** You are born proficient in certain things. If your ability is in public speaking, as mine has been, then that ability has a history within itself. Every time I stand up to give a speech I am drawing on abilities and experience that goes back through the centuries. If you have talents or abilities in woodworking, clerical work, law, gardening, look at legal history, gardens of the world, for clues of where you interests or abilities may have originated.

2. **Everyone is conscious of déjà vu.** Interests, passions, obsessions have a history in a past life or several past lives that you have lived. Build on it. Take advantage of it. You can have a better understanding and appreciation of who you are now, if you realize that this comes from a past time in history.

3. **Even your weaker points,** like indecision, can be understood better, when you see their origins in a past life. When I read about Cicero, I was not only impressed and awed by the extent of his achievements, but even more so, I was impressed by his humanity. I am impressed even by his indecisiveness at certain key times. It was very human. As I came to understand his, in the context of his life, I saw it a result of his trying so desperately to do the right thing—to live the good life, and to live unselfishly for his country. The values espoused at the end of the film, *Gladiator* could be said of Cicero. He tried to live his life FOR Rome—FOR something higher than himself. He lived to express his ideals. His resistance to compromise, which often got him into trouble, was just an effort to do the right thing.

4. **Dreams may have their origins in these past life adventures.** As I read about Cicero's flight to escape death at the end of his lifetime, I was reminded of fleeing nightmares I have had. I was told by a close friend that all his dreams are fleeing nightmares. A knowledge

of past lives might enable us better to understanding memories—pleasant and unpleasant—that have shaped our anxieties, our hopes, and our dreams. Submerged, just below our level of consciousness, is an untapped resource of knowledge of our past and a key to our future.

6

And once again some great Achilles to some Troy be sent

After having seen the incredible similarities between Alciabides and Alexander the Great, and the logical succession of Cicero to the talents and mission of Plato, I began to conclude that there would be a direct lineage of these spirits to the present day. It was not an accident that Alexander saw the legendary Achilles as his inspiration, life-model and hero. I was concluding that not only was he a genetic, physiological heir through his mother, but the living reincarnation of Achilles as well. He "remembered" as Plato would have said, the skills, tactics, and glory of Achilles. They were not only in his heart, but in his spirit memory bank as well.

With three persons in ancient history in this Spirit line—Achilles, Alcibiades and Alexander, I then began to search for someone in a future lineage who would reflect a repressed memory of them in their actions or words. Who else in subsequent history would be walking over the faded footprints of these heroes?

The answer came to my mind, but it was not one I expected. The answer was not a real person, but a person of fictional legend and literature. Who walked on these faded footprints of Achilles, Alcibiades and Alexander? None other that the legendary founder of Rome—Aeneas. He was made immortal in the literary masterpiece of Virgil: *The Aeneid.*

Virgil himself was no swashbuckler, no general, no commander of troops. Virgil's life was devoted to his poetry. He was consumed with studies connected to it. His health was never dynamic, and he played no part in the military or the political life of the country. It is said that he spoke in the law courts one time but without any great distinction and that his shy and retiring nature caused him to give up any ideas he might have had of taking part in the world's affairs.

But the *Aeneid* gives a front row description of the new swashbuckler and world conqueror of a new generation: Aeneas. From whence came these incredibly vivid accounts from this shy retiring, sickly poet? They came from his own memory of his own past lives. Artists frequently wonder from whence comes their inspirations or their new ideas...their story lines, their talent at writing or creating ideas. *They remember.*

A spiritual lineage was developing: Starting with Achilles, role model and inspiration for Alexander, then Alcibiades, then Alexander, then Virgil, remembering his exploits as Alcibiades and Alexander and recording them in his fictional Aeneas. Most recently these behaviors were manifested in Arthur Rimbaud, showing all the passion of Alcibiades and Alexander in his early teen years as he had in these previous lifetimes. Something significant had happened. Somewhere between Alexander and Virgil, he had evolved from a man of action, to a literary artist remembering and recording that action. That continued through Rimbaud. I found myself asking, "What other writer might he have been in between?

This great spirit seemed to have progressed from these incredible giants of action to men of arts and letters. Alexander had lived from 356 B. C. to 323 B. C., and then Virgil lived from 70 B. C. to 19 B. C. I have long concluded there would be lifetimes between this military giant and this sensitive poetic giant. But who would they have been? Perhaps individuals quietly out of the mainstream, making adjustments with each lifetime. I would not be surprised if these lifetimes had been spent quietly on some farm, or as a shepherd or in a library as a minor scholar pouring over historians' accounts of the ancient world.

From the robust Alexander to the sickly poet that Virgil was would have been a huge adjustment. And cramming all that energy (and memory) into one fragile body may have been done on purpose, since the writings of Virgil have influence the world ever since. I came also to see similarities of health problems in Rimbaud and the present day Alex as well. I was later to find a lifetime between them as Cherokee John Ridge, where the same health problems persisted. In looking at the three lifetimes—Virgil/Rimbaud/Alex—we see much creative energy crammed into the early years. Rimbaud seems to have crammed his energies into his first 19 years, and then spent the remainder of his years trying to be a successful businessman—having accepted the values of his mother. Historical accounts suggest that Rimbaud was planning to return to France from Africa and find a wife (to please his mother), and that before he died he converted to Catholicism (to please his sister).

Increasingly, as I have studied each successive lifetime, it seems that our lives are a mosaic. For a few years we may exhibit traits of one previous lifetime, and then for the next few years another. These "periods" of reliving or focusing on the restatement of a previous lifetime's mission, may fluctuate depending on the overall purpose and activity of the soul group.

In my own experience, I paused at the end of Phase II of my life in which I had completed my mission connected with the previous lifetime of Elias Boudinot, and was ready to pass the torch on to other younger members of my soul group. I realized that they were not ready to receive it and move forward. This generation had been ravaged by fears centering around the AIDS crisis starting around 1981. Also, according to Christiana Hoff Sommers in her book, *War Against Boys: How Misguided Feminism is Harming our Young Men* and by Lionel Tiger in his book *The Decline of Males* some feminist organizations have sought to change the curriculum in the schools. They are attempting to create the impressions that there is something wrong with being a male. Some radical feminists have labeled boyhood a male disease.

Quite obviously, this has had a profound affect on some males in this generation, leaving them with the feeling that "There is something wrong with me," and severely damaging their self confidence. In one school, I learned about more than 50% of boys are being given medication to calm them down for exhibiting male behavior patterns such as running in the hall, competitiveness in sports, and others. Consequently, many of the younger members of my soul group, have been, at least temporarily, immobilized or distracted. Unexpectedly, I had to regroup and redirect my thinking, and thus move into Phase III which includes the research and writing of this book.

There appears to be a huge dividing line between the generations starting with those born around 1980 or after. Only time will tell. Certainly, if these sociological conditions can have such a profound affect on a present soul group, we can imagine what a war, or civil war, or famine might have on a soul group—in the 200's A. D., for example. Certain individuals may be immobilized and others may step in to meet the soul group mission, and an individual may have to pass on his lifetime. In this case the "pass," resulting in a lifetime which may be disorganized or unproductive, is not just the fault of the individual, but a result of the turmoil or tumult of the family, society, city, state, nation or world into which he is born.

I optimistically believe, however, that even in a "pass" situation, when one is living what he may feel is an uneventful or ordinary life, some growth is taking place, small at it may seem—all toward our goal, as Dr. Brian Weiss states it, of growing in knowledge and love.

Virgil was born in a tumultuous period himself and lived from 70 B. C. until 19 B. C. When he was 20, Julius Caesar's armies swept down from Gaul, and crossed the Rubicon, starting a series of civil wars and tumult which included Juilius Caesar's eventual assassination in the senate, the struggle for power which brought his nephew Octavian, and Antony and Pompey into power. That period of unrest and uncertainty spanned his 20's and 30's and did not end until Virgil was 39, with the victory of Octavian (Augustus Caesar) at Actium. The hatred of civil war and unrest were frequently expressed by both Virgil and the the poet Horace. In Virgil's 40's he witnessed the blossoming of an unprecedent period of peace—the Augustan Age.

The first literary work of Virgil, known for certain to be his, was the *Eclogues*. They are a series of pastoral poems, rich in lush descriptions of nature and mythology. They were composed when Virgil would have been between 28 and 33.

I would like to offer the *Eclogues* in support of the proposition that Arthur Rimbaud was in the spiritual lineage of Virgil—Virgil's spirit occupying Rimbaud's body complete with repressed memories of Virgil's literary works. With Rimbaud's earliest poems, we see his remembering the *Eclogues*. The similarities are so striking, I am surprised studies and comparisons have not been made often, and are the subject of research by academics.

I think memories from past lives are best from birth and in the earliest years. Until about 10, children's minds are filled with imaginary thoughts, daydreams and imaginary friends. These images occur when the child's portals to previous lifetimes are still open and his memories fresh. Parents, teachers and classmates who chide a child for excitement over these vivid "recollections" should realize they are damaging the child's power and resources of imagination. They are hastening the closing of those portals to the spirit life between lives, memories of past lives, and focus on one's life mission in this lifetime.

All such early fantasies, daydreams, and imaginary activity, should be the source of great interest of, and encouragement by parents and teachers. When these stories and images pour out of the child, the adults should take the role of learner and recorder. The child is being virtually a channel (to use the New Age term), an open door to the wonders of spirit life. Too often the child is made to feel guilty, stupid, or strange for having these normal, mental activities. Too often we try to pour the child or student in school into a mold, which a board of adult educators—a long way from this childhood activity of the spirit—determine. At the present time, when some of our best educational institutions are closing down some of their liberal arts programs, for trade school curricula, teaching students how to do (work) instead of how to think, imagination is discouraged almost from the first.

With such a rich and powerful past, it is not surprising that Rimbaud exhibited these very traits as early as 10. When his portal to past life memories would still have been close to the surface, when Rimbaud was 10, he wrote an incredible description of a pastoral scene, rich and lush in imagery.

He described the sun comparing it to a torch, with its fiery body. He described the leaves on the trees and little flowers and the stream at his feet with extraordinary sensitivity. I propose at this early age, Rimbaud was *remembering* what he had written when he was Virgil in the Eclogues. In Rimbaud's *It Was Springtime* and *Credo in Unam*, he was simply subconsciously remembering poetry he had written as Virgil.

It was the unconscious memory and repeating of these words that I heard that day by my former student, Alex, as he sat on the porch at the farm and, filled with excitement he could hardly contain, talked of going to New York and his future life as an artist. When he said that he was so excited he felt like fire was flowing through his veins, neither he nor I realized at the time, the he was subconsciously remembering lines he had written as Arthur Rimbaud when he was 14 in his poem *It Was Springtime.* And it was that event that was to lead me eventually to begin my quest to discover how we could uncover the mystery and knowledge of our past lives.

It is interesting that we can divide Virgil's work into three different periods or phases of his life. My educational odyssey (phase I) was to take me out of the state, region and country, with degree programs at universities, jobs, and travel, broadening be the key ingredient of the phase. Phase II was what I considered the "workhorse" phase founding and developing the fine arts academy at the farm. I am now in Phase III, in which I am writing a book and a screenplay. I realized as I looked at Virgil's phases, divided by his works, how classic both his and my divisions of a lifetime are. The reader, upon reflection, may realize that your life can be divided as well. To put those divisions down on a piece of paper, and evaluate what you achieved during each one, and what you would like to accomplish in the phase your are now in and futures ones, could prove useful. Consider the questions: "Who am I?" and "What should I accomplish in this lifetime?" While editing this chapter, I had the movie *Alexander* playing on television. When I heard it, I stopped and wrote down the words of Alexander when he said, "At the end of life all that matters is what you have done."

In both the early and the later years, the individual is closest to the past or future lifetime. In the earliest pre-school years, the individual may not be taken seriously, and important remembrances may be lost because of the ignorance of adults in failures to recognize their value. Even more wasted are the later years, after 50. These are prime years with not only one's weakening physical capacities opening doors to the spirit residing beneath the outer, now weakening, shell, but one is subconsciously aware that he or she is approaching, inching closer, to that in-between lives spirit world.

The post 50 years also gives one the wealth of a just lived life to add to the subconscious memories of all the previous lifetimes. If one is wisely aware, a person can spend virtually all of Phase II preparing for Phase III, the really productive and important years. Unfortunately, our materialistic society has taught us a value system which suggests that Phase II is the height not the preparation, and Phase III is the decline instead of seeing it as actually the ultimate time of achievement and fulfillment. This is misguided and wrong. During Phase III while the body grows weaker, the spirit grows stronger by the day, and the sensitivity of spirit qualities and entities are at their peaks.

Viewing Virgil in this way, we see that the early period of writing—the Eclogues would reflect pastoral memories of a past life in a lush natural setting, with love abounding in earlier relationships. The middle phase of his life, when he was busy establishing himself among Augustus' ministers, he wrote the Georgics, which reflect the practicality of one's middle life of strongest attachments to mundane and materialistic *things* in the work years.

This leaves the later period of his life, Phase III, to draw from the greatest depths of his past life memories. And here, in his 40's, is where Virgil drew from his deepest memories of the lifetimes of Achilles, Alcibiades and Alexander the Great.

No matter what age, everyone should sit down and look at his life in these three age groups. If you are a parent, sit down and ask your child questions, reverse roles because he knows things you don't. A child prior to ten has memories that are not a part of your past or your life together in this lifetime. He may still be in touch with the plan for his life, which he decided before he was born with his soul group and be able to remember it. Encourage this *remembering*. Inquire about it. Since you bear the responsibility as a parent for bringing your child into the world, then you should view yourself as the booster on your child's rocket. According to New Age writers, your child chose you to be his parent, because you are supposed to have the foresight and resources to help him realize his mission in this lifetime. I've seen parents, instead, who act like their children are their personal objects and try to use them to realize their own failed ambitions. They are trying to realize fulfillment through their children instead of achieving it through their own efforts.

If you are over 50, realize that you are at your best. You are at your prime to draw from this-life experiences and all previous-life experiences. You should know what is important and what is not. You should be at the height of patience with all those younger than you. You should be sensitive, as never before, to people's (and your own) feelings, thoughts, and needs. I believe that we are all here to help make this a better world, and, simply and basically, to help other people. With each person we see and meet each day, we should be asking ourselves: "How can I help?"

By the time Virgil was entering into Phase III of his life, the civil wars of Rome were coming to an end, and he decided he was ready to write what he had considered the highest form of writing: the epic poem. He decided it would be the *Aeneid,* the story of the founding of Rome, from which the empire would later spring. With memories of the Greek hero Achilles, he created a fictitious exiled Trojan Prince, Aeneas, the fictitious exiled Trojan Prince, Aeneas, the mythical founder of Rome. The theme he chose gave him two great advantages: its date and the subject were close to those of Homer's *Iliad* and *Odys-*

sey. He could refashion events and characters from his Greek predecessor; and it could be brought into relationship with his contemporary Augustan world if he presented Aeneas as the prototype of the Roman way of life. Virgil, in the sixth book, has Aeneas visiting the underworld. There the figures of heroes from Roman history yet to be born pass before his eyes.

The ghost of his father, Anchises, describes them, and the second ends by defining the Roman mission. He sees it as one concerned with government and civilization…'Rule the people with your sway, spare the conquered, and war down the proud:' this is the vision of Rome's destiny that the emperor Augustus and the poet Virgil had before them. Rome was divinely appointed to conquer the world and then spread civilization, according to Roman law, among the people. How more like Alexander the Great, with his mission to bring the wonders of Greek civilization to the far corners of the earth and Hellenize the world, can this be?

The epic the *Aeneid* is a major monument to the national achievements and ideals of the Augustan Age of Rome. The *Aeneid* comes from the voice of a lonely poet, who knew tears as well as glory. This description of Virgil could be applied to Rimbaud as well.

Virgil worked on the Aeneid for 11 years. He had planned to work on revisions of his epic for three more years, but in 19 B. C., he set out on a voyage in the Aegean Sea, to gain fresh insight. He was moving again over the faded footprints of his past lives to the places he was describing in the *Aeneid.* But here, he caught a fever, and left to return home. Shortly after his arrival in Italy at Brundisium, he died.

Shortly before I had starting researching Virgil, the contemporary Alex, had made a trip to Prague in the Czech Republic. He had read that it was the Left Bank of the '90's, as Paris had been a century before. After spending more than week in a student hostel in Prague, near the Vlatava River, he prepared on his final day to return home. That last night he began a conversation with a fellow art student, who, before dawn, persuaded him not to return to the United States, but go with him, instead to Greece. So, on the spur of the moment, Alex changed his plans and went to Greece, travelling across the country and the Aegean, and while staying near the ruins of Ephesus on the Aegean Coast of present day Turkey, he developed a case of food poisoning and became very ill. This unexpected illness caused him to end his trip at that point and return home.

When later discussing with Alex the trip of Virgil to the Aegean, and his becoming ill as well, I proposed to Alex, that his artist friend in Prague that night might have acted as an agent by encouraging and accompanying him to make that journey. The journey had led him over the faded footprints, where he would have traveled before, when he was Virgil in a previous lifetime.

In Virgil's life and work we see one of the best examples in a single lifetime of the use and application of a progression of previous lifetimes. He drew dramatically and efficiently and well, from his memories of Achilles/Alcibiades/Alexander the Great—to produce one of the greatest literary works of all time in the *Aeneid*. At the same time, in his descriptions of the underworld, he was laying the groundwork for literary images yet to come and to be used in his next lifetime as Dante, where Dante even used Virgil as his navigator through the underworld. Dante did not only remember his previous lifetime, but gave credit to it as well.

In addition, Virgil gives us a blueprint for how to organize our own lives into distinct phases, drawing from the new self in each lifetime, we pass through in the early, middle, and later years of our lives. The whole concept of a single life in a single lifetime is fallacious. Each individual lifetime is a mosaic of memories and strengths drawn from successive period of knowledge of these different past lives.

We could apply to this mosaic of ongoing life missions, the sentence from Virgil's Eclogue IV where he says that we weave ages into life as it unfolds, or as we run. We are weaving old lifetimes into the present one, *as we run*, as well as preparing for the next one.

LESSONS LEARNED—CHAPTER SIX

1. **Study events of the period of history in which we live and how they have affected our mission in this lifetime.** Virgil's early years were at a time of civil war and unrest, but his last decade was a time of peace. His work not only reflected this, but seemed to take advantage of it. Analyze your own economic situation and the world economic situation. What does your economic situation enable you to do?

2. **What does your personality prepare you to do with your life?** Virgil's shy and retiring personality did not prepare him to be a general or politician. But he was equipped for the solitary work of the writer, and his sensitivity gave him the insightful qualities necessary for him to achieve his mission as a great writer. Each person should assess his personality in this lifetime, while trying to discover his unique mission in this lifetime determined before he was born. Your physique, your IQ, your powers of imagination, your ability to express yourself in speech or writing are tools in your hands which you chose before you were born. How did you intend to use them? Only you can figure this out. What you thought was a handicap or limitation may be a condition that happened for the purpose of limiting you or narrowing your options so you would do exactly what you are supposed to do in your mission in this lifetime.

3. **Organize your life into phases and study them.** Virgil's life was nearly perfectly organized into phases. I don't believe Virgil did this on purpose, but it poses for us a model, anyway. What have you accomplished in each phase of your life? When you look at your talents, abilities, what being the son or daughter of your parents has put you into a position to achieve, how well have you achieved it? It is never too late. Some of the greatest works come from artists or writers over 80. Michelangelo designed the dome of the Basilica of St. Peters which is so visible to all who watch Christian Services at the Vatican. Michelangelo was commissioned to be chief architect

for this project by Pope Paul III in 1546 when Michelangelo was 71. He continued in that capacity for the next 18 years until he died in 1564 at 89 by which time the dome was almost completed.

7

The awakening of Virgil by Dante is like an arc of a flame which leaps from one great soul to another.

The degree to which the key fits, as I have developed projected scenarios for the next reincarnation of a suspected successor or predecessor in the spiritual lineage of the person I was researching has, at times, been astonishing even to me. This has led me to suspect that we have a kind of divine spiritual help and guidance once we begin the search. If we are alert enough, we may even recognize that we have been led to begin the search. This was the case with Dante as his life repeats patterns and relationships we have seen in Achilles/Alcibiades/Alexander/Virgil. We see him as his own past person—Virgil—as the "guide," guiding the way through the first two parts of the *Divine Comedy*: *Inferno* and *Purgatorio*.

Dante's use of Virgil is a rich cultural symbol in literature. He uses Virgil as *one who advocates reason*. He is also a historical figure which people are familiar with, and he is presented that way in the *Inferno*. Virgil is associated with Dante's homeland. He is presented as a poet, and the theme of Virgil's epic sounds remarkably similar to that of Dante's.

We see inferences which are thinly veiled. Dante was remembering what he had written as Virgil, and his references to Achilles were yet another remembrance of a past life. The use of Virgil as his guide in the *Divine Comedy*, in the first and second parts, is perhaps the most obvious and classical use of a spiritual past life we have by a writer in literature.

The similarities of style and content of Dante and Virgil are obvious, but Virgil expresses it in secular rather than spiritual terms. Dante had studied Virgil carefully. Dante was praised for having a beautiful style similar to Virgil's, but it was a result of more than study. He was *remembering*. Even if skeptics were to say Dante's style is just similar because he had studied Virgil and was familiar with it, then why did Dante choose Virgil's style over all the other styles he had to choose from?

The study of Dante in terms of his spiritual lineage, is like watching a science fiction movie with its special effects molding and contorting from past to present, preparing for future evolution. There is a certain coldness in Dante, I find. I imagined some of the science fiction contortions like taking on a human form in the film *Stargate,* or werewolves contorting to or from human shape. Eventually, in Dante, in looking for past life traits and characteristics, we can see Achilles/Alcibiades/Alexander/Virgil—all present at various times and in various forms in his life, work and writings,

Dante was born in 1265 in Florence, to which he was devoted his entire life, and died in 1321 in Ravenna. Dante had little to say about his immediate family. His father was not of great importance, and his mother died when he was young, before he was 14. Her name was Bella. Dante's father then married Lapa di Chiarissimo Cialuffi, and they had a son, Francesco, and a daughter, Gaetana. His father died prior to 1283, and about this time Dante married Gemma Donati, to whom he had been engaged since 1277.

Like Virgil, Dante's early years were shaped by civil strife—in Virgil's case the civil wars in Rome, which resulted in the peace brought about by the victory of Augustus. In Dante's case the conflict was between the imperial and papal partisans called the Ghibellines and Guelfs. The antagonisms were destructive and deadly. Alternating back and forth, when one side would win, it would inflict penalties and exile on the other.

The Guelfs, supported by papal and French armies, defeated the Ghibellines at Benevento and expelled them from Florence. This brought about a peace comparable to the defeat by Augustus of his enemies in Virgil's time.

When I began my research on Dante I thought if Dante were a reincarnation of Virgil, and an earlier predecessor to Rimbaud, then there would be an equivalent to Georges Izambard. There would be a teacher and mentor to Dante. So, I began to look for him, having remembered very little about Dante from my studies of him in college. My eyes opened wide as I found him right away in Brunetto Latini. Not only was he the teacher and mentor who influenced Dante, but he fit the pattern I was looking for in Plato's life to the letter.

Dante grew up in an atmosphere of postwar pride, a city eager to extend its political control throughout the whole province. The Florentines compared themselves with Classical Rome and Classical Greece, creating the perfect environment for a new lifetime for Achilles/Alcibiades/Alexander/Virgil. Like Classical Greece, Florence sought to extend its power and role as an intellectual and cultural center as well. The leader of this intellectual ascendancy was a returning exile (like Plato had been), Brunetto Latini.

When in the *Inferno*, Dante describes his encounter with his great teacher, this is not the meeting of one pupil with his master. It is symbolic of an entire generation meeting its mentor. Latini had inflamed a public consciousness in the intellectual life and intellectual pursuits through a wide range of prominent figures in the younger generation. These included not only Dante but Guido Cavalcanti and Forese Donati.

We can see in Latini the spiritual lineage of Plato/Cicero/Latini, and to come the teacher of Rimbaud, Georges Izambard. We can see how

Cicero's talents and personality surface in the life of Latini in this description by the then contemporary historian Giovanni Villani. He characterized him as the "initiator" and "master" in refining the Florentines. He taught them how to speak well, and how to guide their republic according to "political philosophy." On almost every topic of ethics and politics, Latini freely quoted from Cicero and Seneca. He also quoted freely, and often, with quotes from the book of Proverbs. This habit and practice was repeated by Dante. Latini's frequent quotes from the Bible, the writings of Aristotle, Cicero and Seneca, in Latini's work, became a great source of inspiration and use by Dante in his early work. Not only did he have the written work of his master teacher as helpful information, but he had the advantage of his teacher's own words in person, remembering (as Alexander would remember Aristotle) first hand.

Rome presented the most inspiring source of thought. Cicero was seen, as not only espousing, but also practicing the model as the ideal intellectual citizen. (Remember, in Cicero, Plato had a chance to put his theories in *The Republic* and his concept of the benevolent dictator into practice when he was consul.) Also reflecting not only Cicero, but also the Greek ideal of Plato, another element of what Latini talked about was the love of glory—the search for fame as a part of the ideal of excelling which permeated the classical Greek and Roman cultures.

Dante sent his first poem to Cavalcanti, and this became the beginning of a great friendship. We see in this friendship, a comparison to the friendship between Alexander the Great and his life long friend and companion Hephaestion. Cavalcanti fits the friendship, in the way in which Alexander composed a monument to his great friend when he died. Alexander had built a funeral pyre the height of a tall building in the desert. Dante composed a monument to his friend in the *Inferno* of the *Divine Comedy*.

Whereas Virgil sought to interpret the founding of Rome by a mythical hero Aeneas, Dante's world was a Christian one, and his mission was to present a Christian world view of the meaning of life. His greatest work, *The Divine Comedy*, is a Christian vision of man's temporal and eternal destiny.

Here Dante by his Christian interpretation is translating his message, fulfilling his mission in the language (Christian world view) of his day. What was that mission? The mission was to bring culture—civilization—to the world. This was his goal as Alcibiades, but his ego got into the way, as well as his lack of knowing how to get along with other people, which the presence of a father or father figure in his youth might have remedied. He succeeded, however, as Alexander, through force of arms to *civilize* the Western "known" world at that time.

Dante was a poet, a prose writer, literary theorist, political thinker and moral philosopher all rolled into one. He is said to have drawn from Virgil (his own memory) and Cicero and Boethius. Circero and Boethius would have been in the spiritual lineage of Plato, founder of the Academy in Athens and author of the *Dialogues* which put forward and preserved the teachings of Socrates.

Something profound happens in the life (and writing) of Dante, which remains a mystery. In Achilles/Alcibiades/Alexander there was a tremendous loyalty toward and love of male friends. This did not mean that they did not have female friends as well. At the end of his life Alcibiades had pulled himself from the arms of a mistress, when he went outside to fight his assassins to his death. Alexander had married Roxanna, a daughter of the King of Persia.

But what appears to happen with Dante is that he seemed to abandon his friendship and loyalty with his male friends, and became totally enraptured with Beatrice—his female savior. To some degree this may have happened in his later life to Rimbaud. Arthur's creativity flourished during his friendships with male friends from Izambard, to Paul Verlaine, to the wild bohemian poet Germaine Nouveau. But somewhere around 20, Rimbaud decided to pursue the materialism his mother had so strongly advocated from the beginning, and seemingly accepted her question, "What is this (his poetry) good for? What can you buy with it?"

Rimbaud after some wandering, sought to make his material fortune by being a coffee trader in Harrar, in present day Ethiopia. By varying reports he tried having a wife, planned to return to France and get married, and with the encouragement of his sister, joined the Church. The fire of his poetry gone out, he had ceased writing it. In Rimbaud, perhaps we saw a repeat of a pattern in this spiritual lineage, which may have started with Dante?

Dante was not subtle. In the *Divine Comedy*, he ended up putting his male friends in hell. They appeared in part 1—in hell, and in part 2—in purgatory. But in paradise, he has his female savior Beatrice. In some ways, the *Divine Comedy* is a forerunner of modern "date movies." In *Good Will Hunting* and *Wonder Boys*, the male protagonist, wanders around with his male friends, but in the end, follows the female—to California (*Good Will Hunting*) or settles down to a domesticated life with a woman which gives his life meaning (*Wonder Boys*).

The question is, "Who or what in Dante's life is Beatrice in the Divine Comedy based on?" Certainly for the male to capitulate and have a female "guide leading him into paradise" was something new. Would we have had an Achilles warrior, the swashbuckler Alcibides who saved Socrates, and led countless men into battle, or Alexander the Great who conquered the world, and spread Hellenistic civilization to the banks of the Ganges as role models had a woman been leading them?

What we may see here is the beginning of an evolution in what Lionel Tiger calls in his book by that name, *The Decline of Males*. Certainly, not one male figure (Dante) can account for all of mankind from that point to this. But it does raise some interesting questions. If Beatrice is more than one woman, whom Dante knew in his lifetime, then what does she represent? Does this represent women taking over, and *leading* men?

In the *Vita Nuova*, which Dante called his libello, Dante tells of his first sight of Beatrice, when they are nine years of age. In it Dante speaks as a young male swain swooning over his loved one. He speaks of his salutation when they are 18, his efforts to conceal his love for her, and his distress when she withholds her love of him. He strives to rise above her rejections, and idealizes her virtues. He then anticipates her death, and then mourns her death. He temporarily is moved by the temptation of a replacement for Beatrice after her death, but somehow her spirit triumphs, and his loyalty to her vision returns. In the last chapter, Dante seems determined to write about her some sublime message that has never been written about any woman.

Commentators remark how impersonal all this sounds, which leads one to wonder about the authenticity of the real people to fit this fictional account. Another question could be raised: Is Dante presenting a fictional Beatrice, to represent a rising and more powerful view women are assuming within the society and within the Church? The Church, even at this early time, was a supporter of the institution of marriage and charged husbands to be faithful to their wives and families. To this day, I have observed that it is usually the wife, who insists on church membership and attendance, and attaches guilt for failure to attend church. The church becomes an arm of enforcement of the marriage contract, as though it were an instrument for women to use to create guilt among husbands who are not "obedient husbands" and "faithful." Is Eve, in the Judeo-Christian story not "telling" Adam what to do? And he does it. And the next thing he knows he is expelled from the leisurely life in the Garden of Eden, his independence and freedom gone. He is having to work hard to maintain and support the family he now is responsible for. So, from the beginning in the Judeo-Christian point of view, the male-female relationship is defined in heavy different terms from the bonds of male-male friendship.

Could Beatrice represent this female presence growing stronger in the society, representing or being the result of a stronger and growing Church? Could Beatrice be a presence which Dante personalized and said he knew from childhood and then expanded on this fictional person he had brought to life to meet his needs in his fictional narrative?

I found myself facing a new unexpected idea: If women were looking to the Church to support and strengthen their position with their husbands, and males in general, and strengthen their positions in society, had Dante found himself in a dilemma as a writer in this growing female dominated society? Did he find himself losing his male strength, exhibited most mightily in the warriors: Achilles/Alcibiades/Alexander? In Virgil we had seen a weakening of the male of action by his having a weaker male body, but a strengthening of the male in his mental talents and abilities in his effectiveness and achievements as an artist/writer.

In Dante, we see the impact of Western Christianity and the Church on the highly charged male. The result is a male who opens his greatest work by placing all his early male friends in hell! It ends by the personification of Woman as his guide through paradise. This pattern is repeated in Rimbaud who abandoned his early friendships with males, and possibly even Andre Breton, in a later lifetime.

I began to question: "Are we not seeing in this one spirit entity, the story of a weakening male in general?" This evolution could begin with the hunter/gatherer role of the male, who provided food for the family by hunting wild animals, and bringing home food for the family. With the advent of agriculture, the wife could meet the function of provider of food for the family, and the male's role and importance reduced. Slowly that role of the importance of the male has been continually eroding down to the present. The women's liberation movement has provided economic opportunities, making the male not "essential" as the only provider for the family. Single parent families without a male adult figure are increasingly commonplace. Perhaps in Dante, above all others, we see this evolution in one person's lifetime. In Beatrice, we see a woman to whom Dante dedicated most of his poetry and almost all of his life.

Beatrice in real life appears to be Beatrice Portianari, who was the daughter of a noble Florentine family. She married Simone de' Bardi and died at 24. In his writings Dante tells of his meetings with her. He describes her beauty. He talks about her goodness. He dwells on her reactions to him.

This is a dramatic departure from Achilles/Alcibiades/Alexander—all of whom had relations with women, but they all had very strong relationships and bonds with men. With Dante, the consuming attention given to a woman, and moving away from primary relationships with men seems to have been firmly established.

We still see in Dante the "memory" of Virgil in the writing of his *Convivio*, which reflects his political and philosophical system. In it, he makes a defense of the imperial tradition and of the Roman Empire. He also reflects the impact of Christianity and the Church on him and his society, when he introduces the concept of home: the innate desire which influences the soul's urge to return to God. This is brought about by proper education and through examples, teachings and doctrines.

In some ways Dante sees the Church performing the role Virgil had proclaimed for Ceasar Augustus, who had brought about Pax Romana. Dante saw his world needing a comparable influence, and it would be the Church which would provide it. Perhaps this was one of the beginnings of the "civilizing" of the world which led to the brutal conquest of the Americas by the Spanish conquistadors forcing the inhabitants into Western thinking and ways.

Repeating Virgil's excitement over the coming of a strong emperor in Octavian—Caesar Augustus, Dante was filled with excitement over what he thought was the bringing of empire to Italy again. This time it was with a Holy Roman Emperor. It was when Henry, the count of Luxemburg, was elected king of Germany, and in 1309, and when the French pope, Clement V, declared Henry to be the king of the Romans. Henry, the count of Luxemburg, was invited to Rome to be crowned Holy Roman emperor in St. Peter's Basilica.

Italy was ecstatic about having an "emperor," and among the advocates was Dante, who, surely remembering Virgil and Octavian, was excited that such an emperor might bring peace, under religious authority. The idea of "restored peace" is straight out of Virgil. This excitement and enthusiasm led to disappointment, however, when enthusiasm for Henry faded, and the pope himself turned against him. Dante, consequently, was disappointed by the papal insistence on its superiority over the political ruler.

Robert Hollander in his book, *Dante: A Life in Works*, emphasizes the degree to which Dante draws from Virgil to such an extent, that it would almost appear he is endorsing the concept of Dante's spiritual lineage from Virgil.

He claims that one can hardly overestimate the importance of Virgil for Dante. He points out that there can be no doubt of the comparison of Virgil in many aspects of the *Divine Comedy*. He even attributes the inspiration of writing an "epic" poem being the result and inspiration of Virgil upon Dante. Likewise, the appearence of many of the aspects of Dante's "poet strategies" are also credited to Virgil. He even attributed to Dante "prophetic powers," which I would say can be explained by Dante's ability to simply *remember* from his past life as Virgil himself. Think of Dante being the full blown reincarnation of Virgil, *remembering* his experiences and having the knowledge of Virgil perhaps even remembering what he thought and felt when Virgil sat down to write.

Not only was the choice of Virgil as a principal character in Dante's poem significant, it was something of a scandal. The *Aeneid* had been interpreted by Fulgentius, and the author of the commentary attributed to Bernard Silvest. It was clear, however, that Dante was not referring to Virgil in such an academic way. That Dante chose an historical figure to represent a mythological one in the *Divine Comedy* may have seemed puzzling. Such an unusual choice and treatment is all the more significant and perhaps has even more impact in my proposal that Dante was continuing the lifetime and literary accomplishments of Virgil in a new lifetime—a new body, new environment, and a new time in history. Keep in mind that our goal is to refine and reinterpret our message and mission in successive lifetimes, growing in knowledge and love in the process.

When it is cited that a number of Dante's interpreters have been deliberately undercutting Virgil, it shows the degree to which they are in error. From Dante's point of view, at least subconsciously, he would simply be reinterpreting Virgil's message and moving it forward according to Dante's new Christian world view and interpretation. Perhaps more than any other two lifetimes that of Dante and his virtual dependence on Virgil for inspiration is best recognized by historians and critics. Having been converted by perhaps both Christianity and the new feminism evidenced in his crush on and captivation by Beatrice, he is torn between his appreciation and devotion to the pagan poems of Virgil, and his feeling of the need to move on beyond it.

Dante is a good example of the role that each one of us is playing subconsciously. He placed the essence of Virgil's life and mission into his (Dante's) contemporary body for the time frame of this new lifetime he was living—seeing the world from Florence instead of Rome, seeing the world from a Christian influenced and dominated perspective rather than a pagan one. His "job" was to reinterpret the truths of Virgil to a new generation. He was to refine, move forward in history, those kernels of truth—to plant the seeds he had planted as Virgil into new young hearts and minds. Dante is clearly struggling, especially in the *Divine Comedy*, to bring all his past knowledge (and remembrances) to bear on this great work. It is a heavy responsibility. It should be for each one of us.

LESSONS LEARNED—CHAPTER SEVEN

1. **Dante is an ideal example of pulling all your knowledge from a past life or several past lives together, and employing it in your mission in your present lifetime.** In some ways, our lifetime could be compared to a science fiction movie. We are like astronauts, who have landed on a strange planet (don't we all feel that way sometimes?). While we were in space (between lives), we were assigned missions, and went to school (previous lives) to train for the mission we have on this planet now. I like to view our mission on this planet, as our "job"—like the astronaut. Our crew is our soul group, and our crew is here to help us, as soon as we team up together, and get started on our "mission." We are not here to accumulate things for ourselves. We must first realize what our mission is and then get started accomplishing it.

2. **We need to find our soul group, or figure out who they are.** James Redfield in *The Celestine Prophecy* gives a good description of what it is like to meet up with our soul group. He says we may be sitting at a restaurant and see someone across the way who looks familiar to us. We may be led to speak to that person, or keep seeing them again until we do. None of this is by chance. It is a coincidence, but all coincidences are by design. Once our soul group is assembled, perhaps composed of some family members, some friends, and others we may meet professionally, then we are ready to accomplish our mission (do our "job"), in this lifetime. That is why it is so important to learn our past lives. "Past is Prologue."

3. **The essence of who we are is an Eternal Spirit.** We should be subconsciously doing two things at once: (1) remembering from the past, and (2) learning from the present. I have consistently urged my students in the past not to live a life set out for them by their parents, family, teachers, spouses, small town leaders. While being appreciative of these efforts, and showing all due respect, each person must seek first to discover who he is. If it takes you half your

life to find out, take half your life. If it takes 90% of your life, take 90%. It is better to take that time, and live just 10% of your life the way you are supposed to, than to spend 100% of your life, living the life someone else has chosen for you. If you do this latter, you have never lived. You have just been a puppet on someone's string in someone else's puppet show.

4. **Your bravest act may be to say no.** No to your family or friends, who want you to live an ordinary, traditional or comfortable life. If after weeks, months, years, decades of searching to find out who you are and who you have been throughout the eternity that your Spirit has been alive, and that your mission in this particular life-time is to live an ordinary life, then do it with joy and happiness. But on the other hand, if the mission of your Eternal Spirit, while it resides in your present body, in this present place and time, is to live like a Van Gogh, or Joan of Arc, or Christopher Columbus, or Albert Einstein, then DO IT. The important thing is to know who you are, why you have been placed on the planet earth in this body, and to know that every day you are standing in your beam, a beam with your body on the one end, and God, the creator of the uni-verse, on the other.

8

Lorenzo the Mangnificent invited artists, writers and scholars to his villas. They discussed ideas and read aloud to each other, listened to music and discussed philosophy. They discussed such matters as man's highest vocation, the nature of the summum bonum and the philosophic doctrines found in the *Aeneid*. With them were a group of friends and members of the Platonic Academy including Marsilio Ficino.

As a student at the University of Georgia, my intellectual growth was reflected in the evolution of my interests. This was indicated by the number of times I changed my major course of study. I began by majoring in secondary education. My very first education course surpassed all academic experiences I have ever had before or since in sheer boredom. So appalled was I by the lack of challenge to my intelligence, that I promptly decided not to major in secondary education and did not take another education course during my undergraduate years. I changed my major to history. After taking one elective course in philosophy, I was so intrigued by it that I pursued history *and* philosophy as a double major. In taking another elective, this time in religion, I was ready to try for a triple major, and concluded my undergraduate study one course shy of having a triple major in history, philosophy and religion.

My first course in religion introduced me to Epictetus (55–135 A.D.). He was a former slave, whose philosophy followed the line of stoicism, but served to introduce the ideas of Plato to the early Christian community. His *Enchiridion*, or manual, was not written by him, however, it was written by Flavius Arrian (b. 108 A.D.). He became an intimate of Hadrian, who made him consul in 130 A.D.

I was inexplicably enthralled by the *Enchiridion* and consequently fascinated by the teachings of Epictetus. I asked my instructor if I could write a term paper on Epictetus and the *Enchiridion*, which I saved for many years. It would have been Flavius Arrian, however, who would be in the spiritual line of Plato who wrote it. Epictetus would have been in the role of the teacher Socrates, who wrote down nothing as far as we know. Like Socrates, Epictetus had his teachings written down and preserved by a loyal disciple. As I reviewed my mysterious and intense fascination in college with this document, I was now looking at Epictetus' Enchiridion written by Flavius Arrian as possibly being a reinterpretation for a succeeding generation of the Socrates' Dialogues written by Plato, Arrian having been Plato in a past lifetime. Was Arrian simply repeating in this lifetime, reinterpreting, refining what he has done as Plato in his past life? I was also asking, "Could I have been so preoccupied by this document because I would have *remembered?*" Could I have been Flavius Arrian in that past lifetime and written it myself? Is that why it so fascinated me, and it felt so familiar and comfortable to me—they would have been words that I wrote down?" Flavius Arrian being made consul would also put him in the lineage of Plato, because as Cicero, he was made consul of the Roman Empire as well.

Following this addition to the lineage of Plato, and following my research on Dante, I was looking into key periods of history for literary figures who would have followed in the footsteps of Plato, and those of Alexander (first as military leader then as literary figure). I did not have to look far. Among the House of Medici in Florence, I found a successor to Plato (writer), Cicero (rhetoric teacher, consul) and Flavius Arrian (who like Plato with his dialogues wrote down the teachings of his mentor). He would have come through lifetimes in the bodies of Boethius and Brunetto Latini, Dante's rhetoric teacher and friend. In the House of Medici, I found him in Marsilio Ficino (1449–1492), who translated all of Plato from Greek into Latin.

Marsilio was the son of the physician of Cosimo de' Medici (Pater) (1433–1499), the ruler of Florence at this time. When Cosimo became aware of Marsilio's gifted mind and his discipline, he adopted him as his own son, and commissioned him to translate Plato into Latin, and to establish and lead a Platonic Academy. This was an incredible time in the history of Italy and the history of Europe. Italy vaguely resembled Greece in the time of Plato, where communities operated as a "city state." There was some rivalry between Florence and Milan, and we might even compare this to the rivalry between Athens and Sparta 2,000 years before. It provided an ideal setting for the reemergence of Plato and Alcibiades/Alexander in a future lifetime and to redefine and refine the divine messages which were their missions to deliver.

Marsilio Ficino, the son of Cosimo's physician whom Cosimo adopted, becomes another role model for all of us to study. New Age writers tell us that we choose our parents before we are born, based on their positions, places where they live, and people they know, to enable us to fulfill our missions in our new lifetime. To be born the son of the doctor to one of the grandest members of the Medici household, was a good choice for Ficino. Being the adopted son of Cosimo also meant he did not have to be concerned with financial matters—responsibilities which would have distracted him for the purpose he had in mind before he was born. He had all the advantages he would have had had he been born a real son of Cosimo, perhaps more, because he had been selected by Cosimo for what must have been a group mission—the founding of a Platonic Academy in Florence.

Rarely, if ever, has this mission from one lifetime to the next been so clearly seen or stated—Fincino's purpose, now his job and title, was to refine and reinterpret to his generation, the essential truths of Plato's dialogues. To do this, he had to (1) remember everything he could from his original writing of them, which would no doubt aid him in his interpretation, but he also had to be learned in the world into which he had been born. He had to speak the language of the "present" generation.

Here again, we have a model for our own lives. To come to terms with our purpose in this lifetime, each one of us needs to be able to (1) *remember* our past lives, know who we were, what we accomplished, where we lived, what our professions were. All of this "knowledge" adds to our ability to function properly in this lifetime—to *fulfill* our purpose in this lifetime. And (2) we need to get all the education we can in the *present* time based on the purpose for our lives in the *present* time.

My "plan" for my life, which I developed when I was 22, I have always remembered word-for-word. It was to "go to the cultural centers of the world, get into the best universities I could, travel, hold a variety of jobs, and absorb culture like a sponge—in short to "deprovincialize" myself." I thought this preparation was for Phase II of my life, but now I realize, it was for Phase III. That includes writing this book. So, even without remembering all the details, I was remembering the most important part—how to prepare myself for my future mission.

Cosimo de' Medici was founder of one of the lines of the Medici family that ruled in Florence from 1434 to 1537. Gaining power by representing the Medici bank, he soon amassed a fortune that made him the wealthiest man of his time. He balanced this with "popular" policies, which made him intolerable to his enemies. He reversed an attempted coup, by bribes and gifts getting a sentence reduced to banishment, and was received like a king when he retired to Padua and Venice. He had elections doctored, and returned triumphantly to Florence, where his enemies went into exile never to return.

Cosimo formed an alliance to crush a rising opposition by a coup d'etat in August 1458. He created a senate composed of 100 loyal supporters. Much of his establishing of power was done to make it possible for him to carry out a building program in Florence. He assembled artists, who were considered simply workers in those days, and made them friends. These included sculptors Ghiberti and Donatello, and painters Andrea del Castagno, Fra Angelico, and Benozzo Gozzoli.

Not only was Cosimo a patron of the arts, but he sought to position Florence as an intellectual capital as well. He organized a search for ancient manuscripts, within and outside the Christian Church. He established a library named for his grandson (the Laurenziana) and employed persons to copy the ancient manuscripts and disseminate them in scholarly editions. Among the copiers were Poggio and Marsilio Ficino.

In 1439, he succeeded in enticing the ecumenical council from Ferrara to Florence. Thus, the Council of Florence, was Cosimo's most important success in foreign relations. The Council of Ferrara-Florence (1438–45) was designed to reunite the Latin and Greek churches to try to prevent the encroachment of Ottoman Turks on Constantinople. Cosimo persuaded one of the main speakers, George Gemistus Plethon, to come to Florence. Plethon was a Byzantine philosopher and humanist, who had sought to clarify the difference between the thought of Plato and Aristotle. But Plethon was more concerned with the advance of Neoplatonic philosophy than with religious questions. His treatise "On the Difference Between Aristotle and Plato" was presented at the Council. This work fired up the humanists and inspired Cosimo de' Medici. As a result Cosimo was led to found the Platonic Academy of Florence.

Not only was Plethon credited with inspiring Cosimo to found the Platonic Academy, but he also introduced the Geography of Strabo to the West. This resulted in the overthrow of Ptolomy's incorrect view on the geography of the earth, and the resulting new theories on the planet ultimately affected the Renaissance concept of the geography of the Earth, enabling the discovery of America by Christopher Columbus.

Cosimo had enthusiastically attended the lectures of Plethon, one of many Greek scholars to speak at the Council of Ferrara-Florence, and at the age of 50 became an enthusiastic admirer of Plato. He virtually recreated Plato's ancient academy in his villa of Careggi, and he comissioned Marsilio Ficino to head it. Cosimo added to his efforts to make Florence a center of intellectual growth by resuming the teaching of Greek at the University of Florence. Greek had been unknown in the West at that point for 700 years. Cosimo, thus became one of the leading influences of humanism.

When Cosimo was inspired to found a Platonic Academy, the logical choice for a head was Marsilio Ficino. Ficino's work in the translating of Plato's dialogues from Greek into Latin, helped stimulate a Florentine Platonist Renaissance. The movement influenced European thought for two centuries.

Ficino had been influenced by Augustine (5th Century) and the leading medieval scholar Thomas Aquinas. When he turned his thinking to Plato much of his emphasis was to integrate Greek thought with Christian theology. (It is not surprising that much of my work in studying religion at the University of Georgia and at Yale University Divinity School focused on Augustine and Thomas Aquinas.)

Ficino became head of the Platonic Academy in Florence in 1462. The library there was endowed with many Greek manuscipts, and it became one of the leading intellectual centers of Europe. In translating the complete works of Plato from Greek into Latin, and the complete works of the Third Century Neoplatonist Plotinus, Ficino was a model for all of us to study. Ficino was simply *remembering* what he had written before as Plato and now Plotinus it seemed, and he was *refining and redefining* for a new generation the message, which he had born before in the bodies of Plato and Plotinus. His work served as a *translation* of this eternal message into the language of the Renaissance, meaning it had the slant of the humanists during this period in Florence. Thus, he was conscious, (as I am trying to be in writing a screenplay aimed at a contemporary audience of people in their 20's.), of his contemporaries. This means I am not only using "film" as a language for the contemporary "translation" of the dialogues, but by studying other films, present it within the context of what young adults are seeing in other films. By adhering to the humanists' perspective, Marsilio was in a similar way trying to speak in the language of his generation.

When Ficino finished the translation of Plato in 1470, and when it was printed in 1484, it was the first complete translation of Plato into any European language. His translations of Plato and Plotinus remained in use throughout Europe for the next 300 years.

When we study the evolution of the spiritual lineage of Plato-Plotinus-Ficino, we can see the familiar characteristics in each. Plotinus (205–270 A.D.), lived in third century Rome, and was at the center of a group of intellectuals. He is considered the founder of the Neoplatonic school of thought. At first glimpse, one might suppose that Porphyry, who wrote the *Enneads*, a book about the writings of Plotinus would be the one in the lineage. There is a kind of hero worship in his writings, and Plotinus himself did not write down that much. So, one might ask, "Was Plotinus in the lineage of Socrates rather than Plato?" But when one looks at Plotinus as a whole, the comparisons lean to Plato.

Plotinus was born in 205 AD in Lycopolis in Egypt. He is said to have had a Greek education, but at the age of 27 he went to Alexandria, where he attended lectures of the most eminent professors in Alexandria at the time. Having heard them, realizing these were the eminent professors of his day, he was reduced to depression. But a friend understood what he was looking for in a learned man, and took him to hear the self-taught philosopher Ammonius "Saccas." This philosopher, I would contend, would have been Socrates in a previous lifetime, *remembering* and repeating, refining his earlier teachings now as Ammonius "Saccas." Plotinus is quoted as having said, "This is the man I was looking for." He stayed with him and studied with him for 11 years. This would be comparable to Plato, who stayed with Socrates and studied with him for 9 years.

Ammonius "Saccas" also attracted the great Christian theologian Origen, and though it was said that he taught a commonplace kind of Platonism, it would be the natural knowledge—*the remembering*—of the teachings of Socrates, that would have come straight from the mind of Ammonius "Saccas" which would have attracted both Plotinus and Origen. Indications are that one did not take a course under Ammonius "Saccas" but, like the followers of Socrates, one sought to be with the sage and follow him to gain as much wisdom as possible by listening to him and being in his presence.

Following his time with Ammonius "Saccas" Plotinus took part in an expedition of the Roman emperor Gordian III against Persia which began in 242. Like the unpredictable and dangerous expeditions of Plato in the Mediterranean, Plontonius' mission ended in disaster, when Gordian was murdered by soldiers loyal to Philip the Arabian who was proclaimed emperor. Plotinus escaped a potentially disastrous situation and fled to Antioch. From there he went to Rome, where he settled down at the age of 40. Porphyry (his biographer and admirer) found him in Rome 19 years later, surrounded by a circle and friends and disciples. We must ask, "Was this not the equivalent of the Academy of Plato, and the Platonic Academy of Ficino?

Plotinus' house in Rome was said to be "full of young lads and maidens," for whom he had been made guardian by their parents. He was said to be arbitrator in disputes and appointed guardian of children in their parents' wills. When he became friends of the Roman Emperior Gallienus (who reigned 253–268), he is said to have asked him to restore a ruined city in Campania and endow it with the surrounding land and name it "Platonopolis." Its citizens were to abide by the ideals of Plato. Plotinus promised to go and live there with his friends.

Here again in this focus on Plato, we see Plotonius trying to establish Plato's idealized city described in *The Republic*, with Plato in his new lifetime as Plotinus functioning as the benevolent dictator. He had tried his hand at this as Cicero, when Cicero was made Consul in Rome. But the emperor Gallienus refused his request, perhaps he himself having been either Julius Caesar or his nephew in a past lifetime. Gallienus had enemies in the senate, and he feared such a community led by Plotinus might be a center of intrigue against him.

Like Plato with his Academy, the main and most important function to Plotinus was his teaching. In his "classes," he would have sections read from the commentaries on Plato or Aristotle, and then expound his own views. No doubt, whether he was conscious of it or not, he was *correcting* the commentaries made by those who followed Plato and Aristotle. The "school" of Plotinus was not well organized. It was a loose circle of friends and people who admired him and came to listen to him speak and teach. There was no corporate organization. It seems that some of his writings, arranged as the *Emmeads* by Porphyry, were very esoteric and intended for those closest to him in intellectual awareness. These included Amelius Gentilianus, who was from Tuscany, and Eustochius, who was his physician.

Plotinus' religion, which he practiced and taught, with calm resolution, was a quest for a kind of mystical union with "the Good." This was to be achieved through the exercise of pure intelligence.

Standing in the spiritual lineage of Plato and Plotinus was Marsilio Ficino, who also gathered his friends around him in an informal discussion of ideas and also in his home, the Villa Careggi, which was the home of the Platonic Academy of Florence.

It was the grandson of Cosimo de' Medici, Lorenzo the Magnificent, who stood in the spiritual line of Achilles/Alcibiades/Alexander the Great/Virgil/Dante. And it was predicable in my research, when I discovered that my projected scenario fit perfectly. Who would and should have been the teacher (the tutor) of Lorenzo? It turned out to be Marsilio Ficino, of course, who stood in the spiritual line of Plato/Cicero/Plotinus/Latini. I was fully projecting into the future as well, when Georges Izambard would be the teacher of Arthur Rimbaud. The seeds that that little frail figure, Arthur Rimbaud, would plant in his revolution in poetry would explode into full bloom in the Surrealist Movement in art.

One cannot read about Lorenzo the Magnificent, without beginning to love him in much the same way one begins to love Arthur Rimbaud. Here is not only the passion of the artist, but the *compassion* of the artist as well.

Lorenzo was the ruler of Florence, but he was also described as a statesman and a patron of the arts and letters. He is considered the most brilliant of the Medici. Lorenzo lived from 1449 to 1492. Less than four months after he died, Christopher Columbus set sail on his first voyage to discover the New World. Lorenzo, like his grandfather, established the appearances of constitutional government, but functioned more as a benevolent tyrant in a constitutional republic. Much of his popularity sprang from the parties and festivals that he organized for the citizens of Florence—feasts, wedding receptions, balls, tournaments. They were organized with fanfare to the extent that one can imagine the festivities of Alexander the Great as he partied with his troops across Persia and into India.

A surprising event rocked the life of Lorenzo and provided a chapter straight out of the life of Achilles/Alcibiades/Alexander for the young ruler. There was a conspiracy against the rulers of Florence formed by the Pazzi bank in 1478. They had taken the business affairs of the papacy away from the Medici family. Sixtus IV, his nephew, and Francesco Salviati, the archbishop of Pisa, and the Pazzi decided to murder Lorenzo, and his brother Giuliano, who was ruling with him at that time. The assassination was to take place *in the cathedral during the Easter Mass* on April 26. The plan was for Francesco Salviati, the archbishop of Pisa, to then take over the council of government. Lorenzo's brother Giuliano was murdered in front of the altar, but Lorenzo succeeded in taking refuge in the sacristy. The archbishop accosted the Medici gonfalonier, who responded by having him hanged from a window of the Palazzo Vecchio wearing his episcopal robes.

The people stood by the Medici when they saw what was happening. They seized the conspirators and tore them limb from limb. Pope Sixtus IV ignored the murder of Lorenzo's brother, but focused on the deaths of two priests and threatened reprisals against Florence. He demanded they hand over Lorenzo to him. Florence and its clergy refused.

The situation was critical because Ferdinand I, king of Naples and one of the cruelest rulers of the century, was supporting the papacy. The limited aid Florence might get from Milan and encouragement from the King of France was not enough. In a move straight out of the life of Achilles/Alcibiades/Alexander, Lorenzo threw danger to the wind and went alone to Naples, to see the cruel King Ferdinand. The hardened Ferdinand was shocked by the boldness of the young ruler (in a scene reminiscent of Alcibiades going before the nobleman whom he had insulted, and removing his clothes as he offered his apologies, the nobleman being so shocked that he offered his daughter in marriage). Lorenzo's audacity and courage in presenting himself *alone* to Ferdinand, left Ferdinand disconcerted, possibly even intimidated. He responded by yielding and concluding a peace. The Pope, Sixtus IV, was thereby isolated, and could do nothing but accept the situation.

Lorenzo emerged from the situation a hero with his prestige greatly enhanced. From then on, he was considered wise. With his new prestige he could have made himself a duke. Instead he created a Council of Seventy to rule Florence. His magnanimity amazed Europe, and he was considered to have all the attributes of a sovereign. His main residence, his new villa at Poggio a Caiano, was seen as having the majesty and elegance of a regal palace. While Lorenzo refused titles, and considered himself a simple citizen, the people referred to him as "The Magnificent," a title he himself by his success as a ruler raised to new heights in the public mind.

The Medici family's patronage of artists, architects, and writers rose to greater heights under Lorenzo. He collected valuable ancient texts and turned his villas into libraries and settings for intellectual discussions. This included his villas in Careggi, Fiesole, and Poggio a Caiano. He called gatherings of the Platonic Academy his father had inspired and his teacher Marsilo Ficino headed. The Platonic Academy was a loose assembly or circle of friends (like the friends who gathered loosely around Plotinus) to discuss Platonic ideas and ideals. These included

Ficino, the Humanist Pico della Mirandola, and the friend closest to his heart, Politian (Angelo Poliziano) a friend who had saved his life on the day of the Pazzi Conspiracy.

When Lorenzo's reputation for his lavish hospitality is described, I am reminded of my contemporary friend Alex. A few days before I started work on this chapter, friends were describing Alex's parties, and it was suggested that he have one in the summer as well as his "Rites of Spring," He also had lavish "Halloween" parties. Like Lorenzo Alex bears the burden of all costs himself, far exceeding what he can afford. For several years friends have pitched in to help financially and with the burden of planning and carrying out such festivities. When I attend these functions, I often say to them, "Ah, Lorenzo is alive and well."

Lorenzo's support of artists was outstanding, and whereas he wrote poetry, he considered himself an artist as well. Artists were, at this time, considered mere workers—like a skilled carpenter or plumber in recent times. But Lorenzo treated them as equals and friends. Under his protection was Giuliano da Sangalo, Botticelli, Verrocchio, and Verrocchio's pupil Leonardo Da Vinci. Later Lorenzo opened a school of sculpture in his garden at San Marco. One of the 15-year-old pupils there, Michelangelo, got his attention, and he was brought up in the palace like a son of the family.

The patronage of the arts and philosophy had started with Lorenzo's grandfather Cosimo, who had been inspired when he listened to Pleton's lectures on Plato. While Cosimo had been inspired to found an academy to support Platonic studies, his enthusiasm had lapsed, due to his preoccupation with other matters. It was the enthusiasm of his adopted son Marsilio Ficino which got him back on track, and kept it all going. Ficino had impressed Cosimo from the beginning when he was a medical student. He had inspired Cosimo to pay for his further education and install Ficino in his villa known as Montevecchio to head the circle of friends discussing Platonic ideas. There in the peace of the country, as a young man he studied Greek and translated all of Plato into Latin. And it was Ficino who persuaded the Greek scholar John Argyropoulos to come to Florence in 1456. When Ficino had grown into maturity, Cosimo would call him over to his own villa at Careggi to discuss Platonic ideas far into the night. It was these spontaneous discussions that led to the founding of the Platonic Academy, and it seems dubious that it would have ever gotten off the ground without the enthusiasm of Ficino to fire the further interest of Cosimo.

In his grandson Lorenzo, we see the interest in Plato amplified even more. Lorenzo invited artists, writers and scholars to his villas at Fiesole, Cafaggiolo and Careggi. This group of artists, writers and scholars talked with Lorenzo. They discussed ideas for hours, read aloud to each other, listened to music together. They discussed classical writings and philosophical concepts. Sometimes they met at the Abbey of Camaldoli. There they set a record. For four days in 1468, Lorenzo and Giuiliano discussed an endless list of subjects including man's highest vocation, the nature of the summum bonum and the philosophic doctrines to be found in the *Aeneid*. Members of the Platonic Academy present included Marsilio Ficino, Cristoforo Landino, Leon Battista Alberti and three merchants of intellectual tastes, Almanno Rinuccini, and Donato and Piero Acciaiuoli.

When I first began to explore the possibility that Marsilio Ficino might be in my own spiritual lineage, I was traveling an hour to Atlanta once a week, and having dinner with Alex, where we were discussing these same Platonic ideas. One such discussion started with lunch at 2 p.m. By 7 p.m., we were still going strong, and we decided to order dinner. We concluded the discussion at 10 p.m.—after eight hours of nonstop discussion of ideas. I remember Alex saying as we rose from the table, "Well, I think we set a record." Not quite, because several years later, with another friend, a similar discussion ran 15 hours. When I read of the discussions of the Platonic Academy, which, that time in 1468, lasted for four days, I realized I was just reliving and "remembering" some of the discussions I had been involved in before.

In considered being in a spiritual lineage that might have stretched back to Florence and included Marsilio Ficino, I began to look into my own past for evidence—to prove or disprove my new projected scenario. I remembered at the University of Georgia, in my survey of art history course, among the items that had most attracted my attention, was not Michelangelo's David, which is enshrined in Florence, but what absorbed my interests passionately were Ghiberti's doors at the Baptistry there. Why my intense interest in these doors, which most tourists and visitors hardly notice? Almost instantly in my new research I found an immediate clue. Sculptor Lorenzo Ghiberti (1378–1455) was one of those who had gained the support and patronage of Cosimo de' Medici. The years, and even the patron, were a match.

When Ghiberti first began work on the golden doors of the Baptistry in Florence he was twenty-three. When he finished he was 73. He completed two sets of doors, the latter for the eastern front. They were gilded bronze panels of scenes from the Old Testament. It was very dramatic for all of Florence when they were finally mounted in 1456. For years, decades, the residents of the city had looked forward to their completion. When finished, Michelangelo seeing them completed would stand transfixed in front of them and declare that they were good enough to be the very Gates of Paradise.

The eastern doors were finished 28 years after Ghiberti had started to work on them. In 1456 Ficino was 23, Cosimo was 67. That was the same year Cosimo persuaded Greek scholar John Argyropoulos to come to Florence. With the arrival of Argyropoulos, and the completion of Gheberti's doors *in the same year*, it is not difficult to imagine the excitement and exhilaration Ficino would have felt. Not only would it be possible to imagine Cosimo, Ficino and Argyroopoulos standing together admiring the new doors to the baptistry, it would have been likely. What also would have been likely is the young Ficino being given the commission by Cosimo to host Argyropoulos around Florence. No doubt Cosimo would also have invited Ficino over to his villa at Careggi and discussed Plato far into the night with Argyropoulos and others. One can imagine the excitement of that year to the young Ficino—especially as he stood with other excited Florentines admiring the 28 year long completed project of Ghiberti's doors on the eastern front of the baptistry.

Perhaps it was that day, and the focus of that day, which led me to be excited as a college student studying the art of Florence. It would explain why that work of art would capture my attention and excitement above all other treasures of the city, including Michelangelo's David and the Uffizi art gallery with its rooms full of Boticellis.

The summer after my first year at Yale, I visited Florence as a tourist. After my arrival, I rushed out of my hotel room before unpacking as I searched excitedly to find Gherberti's doors of the baptistry. In my excitement over this work of art above all others in the city, was I subconsciously remembering that day in 1456? I would not be surprised if my very path that day had taken me over the faded footprints of Marsilio Ficino in his excitement to see the completed doors for the first time. Nor would I have been surprised if I had been standing on the very spot where Ficino had stood panting with excitement (as I was) at seeing the "finished" doors for the first time—504 years before.

LESSONS LEARNED—CHAPTER EIGHT

1. **Look for clues to past lives in things you are passionate about.** When I became *passionately* interested in artist Lorenzo Ghiberti's doors on the baptistery in Florence to the exclusion of the other artistic treasures there, while studying art at the University of Georgia, that was unusual. I didn't realize it at the time, but it was a clue to a past life I had lived. That was also a clue concerning a past place and time in my spiritual lineage. Examine passions you have for places, events, occupations, ways you spend your free time. They are clues.

2. **Look for clues in places you visit**. You usually choose places to visit on vacation, or where you work, if you have an option. I was once offered at job as admissions director of a large art school in Los Angeles. I chose not to accept it, or even visit Los Angeles to consider it. Subconsciously, I must have known it would not have been a course to realizing my goals in this lifetime. On the other hand, in 2000 I was studying in Europe at Prague. After a week in Berlin, and a weekend in Copenhagen, I traveled to Oxford to spend two weeks. I had not been aware of it, but suddenly realized I had subconsciously made a point to visit Oxford every time I had been to Europe. I never once had visited Cambridge in England, nor had nor have any interest in doing so. This is an obvious clue that I would have had a past lifetime in Oxford.

3. **Every thought, every decision you make no matter how small, has its origins in your past lives.** Usually we simply overlook such clues and attribute no significance to them. We should instead, view every interest we have as a clue, especially if it is an unusual or inexplicable interest; especially, if it seems "out of context" with other interests, or "makes no sense." If we have lived more than 80 lifetimes, as had the patient of Brian Weiss in *Many Lives, Many Masters,* then we have a wealth of experiences from past lives to remember. The very volume of such memories could be guiding us

every day in choices we make—right down to our favorite programs on television, or the movies we choose to see, or the books we choose to read.

4. **Think of this lifetime as a mission with a course. Study your course so far.**

In Ficino, we see him following the course of (1) remembering, (2) refining, and (3) redefining or translating to his present generation, the message which he had born in other bodies—Plato/Cicero/Plotinus/Latini down through the centuries. Likewise Lorenzo is remembering, refining and redefining his roles and missions from past lives as Achilles/Alcibiades/Alexander/Virgil/Dante. In my research I am often amazed to see my projected scenario so dramatically confirmed, such as when Lorenzo for four days in 1468 discussed among other things philosophic doctrines to be found in the Aeneid in which case Lorenzo was merely remembering what he had written before as Virgil, and, when Lorenzo was described as a poet, his poetry, no doubt, also being remembered from his lifetime as Virgil.

9

Ridge grew eloquent when describing the abuses of his people and the treaties violated.

Three months after I turned eighteen, I was driving on a beautiful Sunday afternoon in May with a friend through Lily Pond, that section of North Georgia, where my grandfather and great-grandfather had lived. I was telling her the story of how my father had been born only a few months after his parents moved from Lily Pond to Dalton, 25 miles to the north. All of his older brothers and sisters—my aunts and uncles, had grown up in Lily Pond and their mother, my grandfather's first wife (he married her sister after she died) was buried at the Salem Baptist Church.

Some of my most pleasant recollections from childhood were picnics, which came at the end of a "cemetery cleaning" at the grave of my grandfather's first wife Hettie in the Salem Baptist Church cemetery. The church and cemetery were just a few feet from the west side of the road, and across the road toward the east, lay railroad tracks, and beyond that a bend of the Oothcaloga Creek in a fenced in pasture. My Aunt Jennie and I would go fishing in the creek, while everyone else was doing all the work clearing away the honeysuckle vines and small shrubs which had grown up around Hettie's grave. My Aunt Jennie's favorite story was about an incident when I would have been about four or five. One time while we were fishing, a cow came up behind us. When I noticed it, I said, "We'd better run Aunt Jennie. There's a cow, and her husband can't be far away."

Once the work of cleaning the cemetery lot was done, we would have a picnic at the church shelter. There was another private family cemetery, nearby where my great-grandfather was buried. Originally, the family cemetery was on the family farm, but it had been sold off years later, and the graves were fenced in at the top of the hill. We would park the car, and have to go through a pasture to get to the enclosed family cemetery. I can still remember, running as fast as I could, because in this case you could see the bull in the pasture, and while he made no threatening movements, I ran nonetheless.

Then we would drive farther south, by the homeplace of my great-grandfather, Bannister O. Bray, who had owned hundreds of acres in peach orchards. He had fought for the Confederacy in "the war" and had walked all the way back home to Georgia from Virginia when it was over. I always thought of him, when seeing Ashley and the other soldiers return to Tara at the end of "the war" in the movie version of *Gone With the Wind*. My great-grandfather had many idiosyncrasies, some probably resulting from the stress of the war. He owned an organ and would sit and play it on the front porch, while singing to the top of his voice. He had a "gang of dogs", but what enchanted me most were stories of his hidden gold.

I'm convinced that these fascinating stories, I was told at an early age by my father and aunts and uncles, helped instill in me the love I have for history. I may even have foreseen that they may have been a necessary part of the background I would have needed to be motivated to do the historical research in this book.

I was recounting all these wonderful and vivid memories to my friend that Sunday afternoon, as we drove first by the church, then the family cemetery, then by my great-grandfather's home, my grandfather's homeplace, and finally we crested the hill, ready to descend and drive by the enchanting Daffodil Farm. It was the home of our Cousin Minnie

Bray Jones, who had developed it as a business cultivating and selling daffodils. Acres and acres of daffodils she had planted stretched across fields and hilltops, disappearing back into the woods. To me there had always been a certain mystique about it. It was almost hidden from the road by two squares of boxwoods, long since overgrown, with a path between them leading up to the front door.

The house was a one and a half story Greek Revival Cottage. It was nestled in a virtual forest of flowering shrubs, tulip trees, and daffodils everywhere. Years later I searched for the best word to describe the place, and the word was without question: "MAGICAL."

As my date and I drove down the tree covered road from the high hill, and then made the gradual rise to the second one, we descended to the point where the house came into view. As the first column came into view, I became alarmed. The house was in horrible condition. It had not been painted for what looked like years. There were weeds grown up in the yard. On the porch was a washing machine, and a clothes line was strung from column to column. Clearly the house and farm were in a state of decay and deterioration. It had been years since I had made one of these memorable pilgrimages to the home sites of my ancestors. I had never really looked at these places with a discerning eye, but as I looked at the farm this time, I knew its deterioration was so bad, it might be sold and/or torn down at any time.

I was horrified and alarmed. I rushed back to Dalton, deposited my date at her home, and rushed to talk with my father. "What was happening?" Why was the farm deteriorating? What had happened to Cousin Minnie? One thing was certain: If something weren't done, and soon, this horticultural and family treasure would be lost forever.

My father took my alarm and pleas seriously, and he contacted a friend of his in Calhoun, the nearest city to the farm, the next day. We found that Cousin Minnie had died, and the farm had been sold at public auction. The buyer had lived there, but he, too, died several years later. His widow then owned the farm, and tenants were living in the main house. It appeared that she was having financial difficulties keeping up the farm, which was 145 acres. This information alarmed me even more, since she might sell the farm out of necessity to someone who didn't value the house or history at all.

At my urging my father had a friend contact her. My heart sank, when he said she responded by saying that she would never sell the farm. "It is the Garden of Eden, and I will never sell it," she had said. I totally understood her love of and passion for the farm, but that did not remove the risk. It might happen that she would have to sell the farm in a financial emergency, even if she didn't plan to or want to.

I begged and pleaded with my father to find a way to buy the farm. He had been interested in buying a farm house on U. S. 41 Highway where Minnie's sister Josie had lived. It was the Rogers plantations. He was disinterested in the Daffodil Farm, because it was on a dirt road well off the highway. "I must find a way," I thought. "There must be a way to interest my father in buying the Daffodil Farm in order to save it."

Four months later I entered the University of Georgia as a freshman. On weekends, on Friday and Saturday nights, while my fraternity brothers were partying at the fraternity house bar, I was in the subbasement of the University of Georgia library, happily surrounded by microfilm machines, researching the history of Daffodil Farm. "There has to be a way to save it," I kept telling myself. I soon discovered that Minnie had inherited the farm from her mother, who became owner when her husband, Minnie's father, William A. Bray, had died in 1888. Then, I made the stunning discovery that before him, his father, a Methodist minister, Rev. Bannister R. Bray, had owned it from 1837 to 1847. From the farm he moved to Atlanta (then called Marthasville) and preached from the stumps there before the first church was built in 1847.

The significance of this new information was that the first family owner was not just Minnie's grandfather, but he was also my father's great-grandfather. I appealed to my father, "It doesn't matter whether you want to buy the farm or not, YOU HAVE TO BUY THE FARM as an OBLIGATION to your ancestors." Every phone call home, every letter home, was filled with these entreaties. Finally, my father had had enough. "All right," he declared. Almost angry, he had an attorney friend contact the owner, and he took me with him to see her. I realized that if his effort failed, my being with him was a way to shut me up, so I wouldn't talk about it anymore. It was all very dramatic. The attorney friend, my father, the lady who owned the farm and I stood in her living room. My father made an offer—$15,000. (It was 1956.) She said she would sell it for $16,000. I was elated, and thought "BUY IT, DAD!" I felt certain they all must have heard me think it. They dickered for some time. Finally, my father grew impatient. He stormed out onto the porch. I was filled with alarm. He turned and told the woman in an angry voice, that he had never bargained with anyone like this over anything in his life. Then he declared that he would give her $15,000 (his offer) and an additional $200 cash, which she could give her daughter who had recently moved into the farm house. "This," he proclaimed, "is my final offer. And if you decline it, I promise you, you'll never hear from me as long as I live."

With this my father turned walked off the porch out to his car got in and slammed the door, leaving me, the attorney friend, and the woman still standing on her front porch. There was nothing to do but go get into the car. I felt like I was dying every step I took on the walkway out of her yard to the car. I had my hand on the door handle of the car, when I heard her yell from the porch, "Mr. Bray!" My heart leapt with joy! I knew the farm was saved!

On May 17, 1956, the farm returned to the Bray family—92 years to the day from when General Sherman's troops passed through the farm on their way to Atlanta during the Civil War. It was also the wedding anniversary date of my father's great-uncle, Wellborn Mitchell Bray for whom he was named. To my surprise, my father spent twice as much money repairing the farm as it cost, and he and my mother moved there to live permanently from 1956 until 1968, commuting to Dalton each day. So the farm became my permanent home during the years I was a student at the University of Georgia. Living there, I was able to explore its 145 acres, most of which I had not seen when my father bought it. I thought its beauty was overwhelming. Cousin Minnie had operated a commercial flower farm—a nursery—on the property. Way back deep in the woods, one could find all sorts of shrubs she had rooted, and cultivated for sale. In addition to 25 acres of daffodils, there were two acres of peonies and flowering pear trees.

I could not believe it, but the pear trees bloomed each year on the very day that most of the daffodil fields beneath them were in full bloom. My father would say, the daffodils bloomed on his birthday—March 23 every year. It took me several years to realize he was right!

During my senior year several weeks apart, both the head of the philosophy department and the head of the religion department at the University of Georgia proposed that I enroll as a student at Yale University Divinity School. They had been students there, and they said they thought I would do well there. It was to Daffodil Farm that I came on the weekends to ponder my future. Finally, concluding that the farm might not have been saved without my efforts, and discovering that it was a resource more spectacular than I had realized, I decided on my future. I would divide my life into the phases (1) my educational odyssey, and (2) return to the farm and use it as an INSTRUMENT to make this a better world for the next generation. The farm, then, became a focus of my life mission.

I returned in 1975 with degrees from Yale and Johns Hopkins in hand, and my travels and broadening educational and professional experiences behind me. From 1977 to 1980, I was Executive Director of the Rome (Georgia) Area Council for the Arts, and in that capacity was elected president of the Georgia Assembly of Community Arts Agencies. I arranged our first Board of Directors' meeting at Hambidge Center, near Dillard, Georgia, specifically because of its profound influence on me. Mary Crovatt Hambidge had been dead for seven years. I had visited her there during her lifetime, and would sit with her on the porch of her mountainside home and listen to her expound on her life with Jay Hambidge, her husband, and the development of his theories of dynamic symmetry. Knowing that I had visited her years before, the Director of the Center for that weekend meeting, assigned me for sleeping quarters, Mrs. Hambidge's house on the mountain side, where she and I had had our long discussions.

At our board meeting of the Georgia Assembly of Community Arts Agencies, I proposed the use of Daffodil Farm for a summer program for high school art and drama students, and the idea was greeted with unanimous enthusiasm. I was urged to form a separate non-profit arts organization to conduct these programs, which I did. Our first summer program took place in 1981 at the Daffodil Farm. Later the program changed to help at-risk inner-city youth and students who were emotionally and behaviorally disabled.

Meanwhile, I continued to have open houses when the daffodils bloomed in an effort to raise some money to help support the program for emotionally and behaviorally disabled students. One year I asked the help of a friend Dan Biggers, the director of Oak Hill, the ancestral home of Martha Berry, founder of Berry College in nearby Rome, to aid us in our refreshments for the open house. Dan was also an actor, who appeared in television films with some regularity. He was the coroner, in the television series, *In the Heat of the Night*, with Carroll O'Connor. This became Dan's first visit to the farm, and he said, "I am ten times more impressed than I thought I would be." He was fascinated by the house, and asked, "When did you say this was built." I said, "It was built in 1837, when my great-great-grandfather came here."

"You're wrong," he said. "The house dates from the 1780's or the 1790's." I was stunned. I said, "But there was nobody here then." Hardly had my mouth gotten out the last word of that sentence did I realize the absurdity of that statement. Of course, somebody was here! The Indians were here! The farm was only nine short miles from New Echota, the capital of the Cherokee Nation, and it was thriving in the 1820's.

Immediately I recalled that there had been a man interested in log houses visiting the farm only a few months before. He had traveled regularly to Kentucky, and would buy old log houses, and dismantle them. He would then ship the logs to Georgia, where they would be used to build new log houses. When he looked at the foundation of one of the chimneys at the farm, he said in awe, "I have never seen a chimney foundation this old." He had estimated that the house had been built in 1790.

I had been so fixed on the belief that my own great-great-grandfather had built the house, that I had ignored other possibilities. Then, I recalled that a friend of mine, a historian from Milledgeville, had explained to me that fireplaces like those in the house, had not appeared after 1820, well before the 1837 date I had given for the building of the house.

Here, then, were three different sources in disagreement with my 1837 date, and all three saying it dated from 1790 or before. There was no question in my mind now. I must have been wrong. Dan and I discussed where I should start my research, and the obvious starting place was New Echota. As soon as they opened the next day, I was there. I found that in 1832, there had been a land lottery, in which the state of Georgia, divided up the Cherokees' property into 160 acre squares, and gave it away to white settlers in other parts of the state. According to a treaty that had been signed, an evaluation was made based on what was on each farm, and the Cherokees were to be paid that amount for their property. The descriptions of those 160 acre squares in this part of Georgia included owners with the description of their house, corn cribs, stables, etc. in each district.

I soon realized that there was still a way to locate a possible Cherokee owner of the farm. What I had to look for was a piece of property whose description of the buildings and pastures in it would match the farm. I excitedly poured through the description of every Cherokee property, in Oothcaloga, the district where farm was located. Oothcaloga was a Cherokee name meaning "place where beavers build dams." White settlers changed the name of the district from Oothcaloga to Lily Pond in 1850. Soon, I found three possibilities—three properties whose main house might fit the house at the farm. They were Isabella Hicks, Archy Rowe and Stand Watie. None of these names meant anything to me. I quickly made copies of the full documents. I took them home. That night at the farm, I started studying the documents more carefully.

When I got to the description of Stand Watie's property, I was reading down the list of out buildings, and what was fenced in. They had to fence in vegetable gardens and yards to keep the wild animals *out*. I read each one: corn crib, stables, vegetable garden, and then as my finger moved down the page, my heart skipped a beat. I paused at the following description: "**Yard and spring lot: 2 acres.**"

That was the farm! I knew it instantly. The house faced a glen with three springs, and around the springs was the yard. Was it 2 acres? In the dark, I ran outside. From the center of the spring area, I walked off an acre—210 feet—in each direction, then across from one side to the other. There is no way it could have been more nearly a perfect "Yard and spring lot—2 acres." In addition, the dimensions of the house fit perfectly. The existing barn was antebellum, but it was clearly made out of logs used in some previous building, since you could see where pegs had fit in before in an earlier building, so it was made probably by tearing down the outbuildings described in Stand Watie's property list.

I could not wait till the next day to phone my friend Dan at the Martha Berry Museum. I told him what I had found. I remembering saying, "Dan, it was owned by some Indian named Stand Watie." There was a long, long pause on the phone, and then Dan said, patiently, "**Bill, your ancestors are but humble caretakers, compared to the Cherokees who lived there.**"

It did not take me long to get back to New Echota to find out who this Stand Watie was. And I was soon at all the regional libraries as well. I was in awe and amazement as the results of my research unfolded over the next two years.

The results of this research indicated that the farm had been built by Oo-watie, brother of Major Ridge. My research revealed that Oo-watie and Major Ridge were descended from King Attakullakulla, the "solon" of the Cherokee Nation. He had been called The Little Carpenter, from his ability to settle disputes. While still a youth, he was known as Ookoonake, or The White Owl. He had gone with Sir Alexander

Cuming to London, where His Majesty King George II had received him along with six other Cherokee chiefs in 1730. This lineage made them connected to such leaders as Old Hop, Dragging Canoe, Nancy Ward, Doublehead, and Old Tassel, as well as Sequoyah, who achieved fame as the inventor of the Cherokee syllabary. In short, this was the royal family of the Cherokee Nation. I was overwhelmed.

It appears that Major Ridge had chosen a homesite on what is now U. S. 41 (which I later realized was the very farm my father had had a passion for buying), and his brother Oo-watie chose this site two miles west. What later was to become my family's cemetery, and where my great-grandfather, and his brother Minnie's father are buried, was a community cemetery, which may have served as the burial place of children of both of these Cherokee leaders. It also appears they both built a Greek Revival Cottage, a later version of the frontier dog-trot house—possibly identical dwellings. Major Ridge's house, which the Rogers family would have lived in following the Cherokee removal, had a second floor added by the time my father had become interested in it.

The Cherokees prided themselves on emulating the white man, and to build a white man's dwelling would have been their ideal. Further up Georgia 225 less than 20 miles from New Echota, at Spring Place Chief Joseph Vann had built a two story "mansion," the envy of any white man in North Georgia.

Oo-watie had two sons born at his home, now the Daffodil Farm, The Buck or Buck Watie, born in 1804, and his second son "Standing on Two Feet", "Stand" for short, or Stand Watie, born in 1806. Buck attended the Moravian School established at Spring Place near the Chief Vann House. But he was so bright, he and a classmate, David Brown, were taken to the best Moravian School in the country in Cornwall, Connecticut.

When I read about this trip, I had already become involved in my reading journey. I had already begun to suspect that things we were doing in this lifetime were *connected* to what we had done in previous lifetimes, perhaps *reliving* them—walking over our own faded footprints.

Buck Watie was 14 when his teacher left Georgia with him to take him to the Moravian School in Connecticut. The missionaries who took him made good use of the journey. They stopped in Charlottesville, Virginia and visited Thomas Jefferson, who was at home at his mountain top home Monticello. It was the year construction was starting on his University of Virginia, which he had designed. President Jefferson had a telescope where he could observe progress and supervise construction from his home, since Monticello was on one hilltop outside of Charlottesville and The University of Virginia was being built on another hilltop just a few miles away. No doubt Mr. Jefferson was brimming with excitement and would have shared this enthusiasm with these visiting young Cherokees.

The purpose of the visit was to show off these bright young students and to make a case that the American Indians were not savages. There was also hope for finanicial support for their program. Even when I visited New Echota a few years ago, one of the interpreters was expounding on how bright Buck Watie was. She said Buck was said to be "one of the brightest men in America—white or red."

Having visited Mr. Jefferson at his magnificent home, they were off again on their trip. They stopped in Washington to visit President Monroe, who was also at home, in the White House. After showing off their two bright young Indian students, the group stopped at Mt. Vernon and visited the tomb of George Washington. From there they continued through Baltimore and Philadelphia to New Jersey, where they stopped off for a visit with Elias Boudinot, the President of the American Bible Society, who had been President of the Continental Congress. This time their visit so impressed their host, that Elias Boudinot insisted that the young Buck Watie adopt his own name in the future.

Undoubtedly the young Buck Watie was suitably impressed with his new older friend himself, because when Buck finally arrived at the Moravian Mission School in Cornwell, Connecticut he signed in, and wrote as his signature for the first time: ELIAS BOUDINOT.

By the time I finished reading this account, chill bumps had begun to run and up and down my spine. During the summer, when I was 14, I had made an unusual request of my parents: Could they take me on a trip to Washington. They wonderfully co-operated with my proposal. We visited the Natural Bridge of Virginia (perhaps that too was visited by the young Buck Watie), Monticello in Charlottesville, Virginia, the White House, and the tomb of George Washington. What an interesting coincidence, I had thought. I was retracing the footsteps of the young Buck Watie at the age he would have been making the trip without knowing it.

At Cornwall, Connecticut, Elias Boudinot fell in love with Harriet Gold, daughter of one of the leading white families of the community. American Indians were still considered savages by most of the town people, and one horrible night, the two of them watched from a window of her house while they were being burned in effigy in the town square.

Buck (now Elias Boudinot) married Harriet Gold, and they returned to Georgia. They lived at the farm with his parents for a year, working not far south of the Daffodil Farm. Eventually he built a new home at New Echota.

Elias Boudinot's first cousin, John Ridge, who had grown up two miles to the east, had also studied at the Moravian Mission School at Cornwall. He, too, returned to Georgia, and had built a home several miles south of New Echota. Stand Watie had attended school at a Moravian Mission School in Chattanooga. He returned to live just north of New Echota, but later, as his father got older, moved back to the Daffodil Farm to look after him, and it is Stand's name which appears on the records as its owner, when the evaluations took place. Major Ridge, his son John, and his nephews—Elias Boudinot and Stand Watie became the leaders of a movement within the Cherokee Nation, which became known as the Treaty Party.

Major Ridge had helped Andrew Jackson become elected President by enabling Jackson earlier to win a major victory over the Creek Indians at the Battle of The Horseshoe Bend. When the rumors circulated that gold was being discovered in north Georgia, white Georgians wanted the land the Cherokees owned, which stretched from present day Atlanta to Chattanooga. Georgia simply passed a law giving the land the Indians owned to white Georgia settlers in the rest of the state. In a land lottery, the Cherokees' property was divided into 160 acre squares. The Cherokees protested and met in their Council House at New Echota, in a government they had modeled after the government of the United States. Instead of war, they took their case to the U. S. Supreme Court, which ruled in favor of the Cherokees. The U. S. Supreme Court ruled that the Cherokees owned their property and that the state of Georgia had no right to take it.

Major Ridge, his son John, and nephews Elias Boudinot and Stand Watie were jubilant. Major Ridge knew that Andrew Jackson owed him a huge debt because of the military victory Major Ridge had enabled Andrew Jackson to win at Horseshoe Bend. Instead, they were all devastated when Andrew Jackson turned his back on his friend, and said, that if John Marshall (Chief Justice of the Supreme Court) wanted to rule in favor of the Cherokees, then let him enforce it.

This meant the President, and hence the U. S. Army, was not going to side with the Supreme Court. As I read accounts of the pleas made to the Congress by these four, and the countless trips they made from north Georgia to Washington, D. C., I was astounded. Elias Boudinot had been made editor of the Cherokee National newspaper, the Cherokee Phoenix. He was also designated to be Director of a National Academy of the Cherokee Nation, but when funds were not available to do both, the leaders opted to have the National Newspaper. He and his cousin, John Ridge, had traveled throughout the Northeast making speeches and seeking support for the Cherokee cause, wherever they could.

But Major Ridge realized that he had been betrayed by Andrew Jackson. He also knew that without the support of the President, their cause was lost. In an effort to salvage what they could, Major Ridge, his son John, and nephews Elias Boudinot and Stand Watie assembled with others at the home of Elias Boudinot at New Echota. There they signed a treaty in which the Cherokees would agree to relinquish their property for payment and willingly move west to Oklahoma. This act was opposed by a rival chief John Ross. John Ross, whose home still stands in Rossville, Georgia, was the son of white traders. As a child he was fascinated by the Cherokees his parents traded with, and since he was one-eighth Cherokee himself, he was able to enter the Cherokee political arena. He ran for chief and was elected.

Earlier in the struggle with Georgia, he and the Ridges had worked side by side. But when Major Ridge and the Treaty Party knew all hope was lost, they counseled what they believed was to be in the best for the Cherokees—get the best deal they could and get out. John Ross on the other hand, counseled the Cherokees not to move. Since a majority did not want to move, they did not attend the meeting where the Treaty was signed at Elias Boudinot's house. While a majority of those present signed, a majority of the total Cherokee population did not attend. Congress approved the Treaty of New Echota, and in March 1837, Major Ridge, his son John, Elias Boudinot and Stand Watie boarded a barge at Ross's Landing in Chattanooga, Tennessee, along with 466 other Cherokees who had accepted payment and agreed to leave for the west. Once in Oklahoma, Major Ridge and his family set up a government and attempted to restore life to some kind of normalcy.

But already in Georgia, white Georgians had begun to terrorize the Cherokees. Some Cherokees had committed suicide. Others were being driven from their homes. In the Spring of 1838, federal troops were sent into the area to gather those who had not yet moved west. Women and children were dragged from their homes, and forced to go to stockades, where they sweltered throughout the summer of 1838. By the end of the summer, the stockades had been filled, and a forced march on foot was begun. That forced march took place throughout the fall and into the winter. In the march which stretched from Georgia to Oklahoma, 4,000—one-third their number—perished along the way, the pathway scattered with unmarked graves.

Once the remnants arrived in Oklahoma, the followers of John Ross announced their intentions to form a new government. The earlier settlers and the Ridge-Watie family leaders had had a leadership already in place for a year and a half—since the arrival of the band of nearly five hundred that had left Georgia in March of 1837.

Ignoring efforts to set up a unified government, on Saturday, June 22, 1839, four squads of assassins loyal to John Ross were sent out. According to all accounts, the violence was well planned and executed. The first group of assassins, some twenty-five men, were said to have been some who had been fed and clothed by the Ridges. This first group reached the house of John Ridge at daybreak. Three assassins sneaked through the house grabbed Ridge and dragged him from bed, and into the yard. John Ridge's wife and children watched and wailed. While two of the executioners held his arms, the others held his body and stabbed him deliberately until 25 wounds pierced his body. They then threw his body into the air as high as they could, and when his bleeding body hit the ground, each murderer stomped on it, marching over it in single file.

The second band, 30 strong, sought out Elias Boudinot. Four of the band sought him out to discharge some medicine which he was in charge of, while he was on his way from a house being built. After they had walked half the distance, one dropped behind and plunged a knife into Boudinot's back. The other swung a tomahawk and split Boudinto's head, and swung it again and again, until his skull had been split in six or seven places.

Major Ridge was murdered by being shot in the back, while he was riding his horse. Elias Boudinot's wife got word to his brother, Stand Watie, and Stand escaped the assassins assigned to him. The enmity between Stand Watie and John Ross continued over the years, and eventually Stand Watie was elected Chief of a Western Branch of the Cherokees there in Oklahoma. During the Civil War, he was became a General in the Confederate Army and was the last to surrender at the end of the War. He was described as the "foremost soldier ever produced by the North American Indians."

When I concluded this research and realized that Elias Boudinot and Stand Watie had both been born and grew up at the house at the Daffodil Farm, I was in awe. No wonder, Dan Biggers, the Director of the

Martha Berry Museum, had said, "Your ancestors are but humble caretakers compared to the Cherokees who lived there."

Some time after this, as I was involved in my "Reading Journey," I was reading Dr. Brian Weiss' comment that some of our birth marks or moles may be remnants of "wounds" from battles in previous lifetimes. Suddenly, it dawned on me that a pronounced birthmark on my back, between my shoulders was exactly that kind of birthmark, Dr. Weiss was describing. It was narrow and long, and ran vertically, almost an inch in length. When I began to wonder, could this birthmark be the kind of remnant of a past life, I had forgotten how the Ridges had died.

I dug out my Cherokee history book. I first read about Major Ridge's death, wondering if my birthmark could have been the wound left by the bullet that killed Major Ridge. Then I read about John Ridge, but 25 stab wounds would have been many more than what my birthmark would indicate. Then I read about Elias Boudinot, and there was a perfect match. He had been stabbed once, in the middle of his back. My birthmark would have been a perfect example of Dr. Brian Weiss's point, if I had been Elias Boudinot in that lifetime. Then I began to look for other clues.

I remembered that at the age of 14 I had mysteriously sought to have my parents make that trip to Washington, which ended up retracing Elias Boudinot's trip when he was 14, stopping at the same places he stopped.

Anything else? In my research, I had discovered that he was the editor of the Cherokee National newspaper, the Cherokee Phoenix. I had been editor of my own newspaper in Baltimore, a weekly to promote Baltimore and the arts in the Washington-Baltimore area. I had had my own weekly column too. Perhaps more important, I had founded an Academy at the farm. I read that Elias Boudinot was supposed to be the Director of an Academy at New Echota for the Cherokee Nation, but when the funds grew short, it was decided that he would devote his entire attention to the newspaper, and the academy would have to wait.

Anything else? I had seen a closeness between Elias Boudinot and his cousin John Ridge. They had gone to the same Moravian School in

Connecticut. And like Elias Boudinot I had gone up and down the East Coast looking for financial support for my venture—the Academy. On one occasion, when they were fighting for the cause of the Cherokees, trying to raise money, they spoke at Clinton Hall in New York. John Ridge's word's were unforgettable and quoted in New York newspapers. Once when I was in New York and having dinner with Alex, who would have been John Ridge in the Cherokee lifetime, we met near Astor Place. According to my research, it would have been near there that John Ridge and Elias Boudinot would have made one of their pleas for financial support. I wondered out loud to Alex, "I wonder we might have met here at this place to have dinner, in that previous lifetime, when we would have been in New York?"

Once I visited a friend in Philadelphia, who lived across the street from the First Presbyterian Church. Later, as I was researching the speeches Elias Boudinot made in support of the Cherokee causes up and down the East Coast, I paused when I read that he had addressed the congregation at the First Presbyterian Church in Philadelphia. I realized that when my friend and I had walked out of his apartment and down the other side of the street, we would have been walking over the faded footprints of Elias Boudinot. I had unknowingly returned to the site of his Philadelphia appearance.

When I discovered on the Daffodil Farm an ancient stickball field, that had been the site of the National Stickball game of the Cherokee Nation in 1825, I began to seek better and more complete descriptions of the event. It had drawn enormous attention. These stickball games were normally drunken festivals, which might go on for days. But this one had gotten unusual attention from the Moravian missionaries because it had been held on Sunday. This drew their ire, because virtually all the participants—which were their entire congregations—were at the stickball game and not in church.

I was searching for the diary of one of the missionaries, Moody Hall, who had written in rage extensively about it, and incredibly found a copy of the document in the Candler School of Theology Library at Emory University in Atlanta. There was also an account in his diaries of a visit he had made to the Moravian Mission School at Brainerd near Chattanooga. It turned out he was the very missionary who had been so shocked at John Ridge throwing off his clothes and leading the other students at recess to jump into the Chickamauga Creek naked.

In the late 1990's a couple of historians spent a day at the farm gathering information about Major Ridge, John Ridge, Elias Boudinot and Stand Watie for an exhibit at a history center in Atlanta. When the exhibit finally opened the next year, I was already living in Atlanta, and I made a point to see it, to see if I had been any help. It was an extensive exhibit.

As I came around a corner, I could not believe what I was seeing when I saw the picture of Elias Boudinot and a page of the Cherokee Phoenix. But what my eyes were fixed on in disbelief was a knife. Yes, it was the very knife with which the assassins stabbed Elias Boudinot in the back on that June morning in 1839. As I stood there staring at it, I imagined the birth mark between my shoulder blades ached.

The similarities between my interests and activities in my life incredibly matched and repeated those of Elias Boudinot. If I were he in a previous lifetime, then the seemingly absurd passion I have had for saving and preserving this farm in north Georgia would make sense. I have spent 44 years of my life devoted to that task—that mission surrounding that single place.

Not only did I use it for two decades to help students, and continue the altruistic use of the farm by these gentle peacemakers of the Cherokee people, but three out of five generations of my family were ministers who lived there. In the process, I had personally saved the farm from destruction three different times. And perhaps the greatest accomplishment, inspired and aided by these restless spirits, was to rediscover the ancient Cherokee history of this Sacred Place and tell their story again.

My devotion and passionate love for this place surpassed any focus I had seen in other people, and it was as much a mystery to me as it was to my friends. As I contemplated a spiritual lineage to Elias Boudinot, seeing all the similarities, then that would explain my extraordinary passion. In my subconscious spiritual memory bank would have been my memories of being there from birth and growing up there. When Elias Boudinot returned to live there with his new wife Harriet Gold, while their house was being built at New Echota, he would have been my age when I discovered the farm was facing destruction. Equivalent to the year he spent there with Harriet, while their house was being built at New Echota, was the year and a half I struggled trying to get my father to buy it in order to save it. My trips up and down those same country roads would have been over his faded footprints, made by him at the same age.

There is even a stretch of road that he would have passed over going to work that year, that I had described many times in my earliest recollections. I had said simply that when I drove that stretch of country road, I felt like I had been there during a previous lifetime. Now I was convinced that I had.

When finally, I had done everything I had known to do to preserve the farm, and use it to help other people, I had to sell it due to my inability to find financial support to operate the educational programs there. As the time came to pack, I remember looking out of the second floor bedroom window toward the driveway. So, overwhelming was the feeling that I had been there and done that before, that I had to abruptly stop and rush down stairs. Only days later, and with a friend did I return to continue. I concluded I would have been remembering packing before in my father's house, in the little attic bedroom, where I would have grown up as Buck Watie. Then we would have been packing for the long trip to Oklahoma. As the pain rolled over me again, it was too overwhelming, too filled with meaning. I realized it was because *I remembered.*

CHAPTER NINE—LESSONS LEARNED

1. **Analyze any passions you have, especially, those which seem unusual or extreme.** The passion I had, and the utter devotion I had, in saving and preserving Daffodil Farm was a mystery to all my friends. How could I be that interested in a farm in the middle of nowhere? It was a mystery to me as well. My friends in high school were so amused that they made up a little song: "We're marching to Lily Pond. Run, Bannister, run." I endured their amusement, even though singing it became a regular feature of "riding around" that my friends and I did after school each day. It was as though I were seized by a giant hand and held fast. Paul Tillich had described religion as "being grasped by an ultimate concern." Was I "grasped?" Yes. Was this devotion and dedication religious? Yes.

2. **Create a map, showing where you have lived.** Study it for clues. After I had been to Yale and Johns Hopkins, lived in New York, Boston, Baltimore, and Oxford, England, the prospect of coming back to a farm in "the middle of nowhere"—halfway between Atlanta and Chattanooga—was as difficult for me to understand as it was for my friends. My life style of choice was living in a high rise apartment in a big city. In New York I had lived in a 22nd floor apartment, which looked out over Central Park. In Cambridge, Massachusetts I had lived in a 7th floor apartment looking out toward the Charles River near Harvard Square. In Baltimore I had lived in a 9th floor apartment looking out over Wyman Park, the Baltimore Museum of Art, and Johns Hopkins University. No yards or upkeep for me. I had lived just a few blocks from Harvard and Johns Hopkins, and in New York I was on a block that had Lincoln Center on one end and Central Park on the other. All of this had been at the center of or on either end of this country's and the world's major MEGALOPOLIS. I had defied all my preferences and life style choices to return to rural Georgia.

3. **What it your mission in this lifetime? It is the most important question of your life.** I was coming back to a 145 acre farm, more than an hour from a major city in the middle of the South. But I was coming back to fulfill a lifetime mission. Did I have any choice? None whatsoever. NONE. I would try to make myself feel better by saying (which was true): If the Lord had wanted me to be in the middle of the jungles of Africa, I would be there. If the Lord wanted me to be up the Amazon, I would be there. If the Lord wanted me in the middle of a desert out West, I would be there. And then, I would say, "Thank you Lord, for putting me to within an hour of a major city." What I did not know then, was that I was following to the letter, a plan that had been worked out before I was born, and the important thing was: I WAS ON SCHEDULE.

10

'We must change life' became a guide for Breton as well and those who followed him in the Surrealist Movement.

It had not taken me long to begin developing a chart, not unlike genealogical charts, showing how the spiritual lineage connected a person's successive lifetimes. By now my chart was showing that the soul group of Elias Boudinot and John Ridge (both of whom died in 1839), was followed by the soul group of Georges Izambard (born 1848) and Arthur Rimbaud (born 1854).

By simple reasoning, I realized that there would have been another soul group and lifetime between Arthur Rimbaud's (who died in 1871) and the present. When I was concluding my research on one group, and ready to turn my attention to this question, I remember having lunch that day with one of my former art students, and telling him where I was going to go next in my research. Without really having thought about it I asked, "Was there a movement in art after Rimbaud's death in 1871?" The look of astonishment covered the face of my luncheon companion. "Yes, of course there was. The Surrealist Movement!" Of course, I gasped. I had really not thought about it, because this is the famous movement of art in Paris which produced Pablo Picasso, Salvador Dali and countless other artists, who were beginning to flourish as the world moved into the Twentieth Century.

The next step was simple enough. I went to the bookstore and bought a book on surrealism. I began to look for a successor in the movement to Alexander/Virgil/Rimbaud—most notably Rimbaud. As I began to read through the pages, I froze when I got to the first Surrealist Manifesto. It was written to one Andre Breton, and again, I found words I had heard before, and as before, out of the mouth of my former student and friend Alex. I had heard them over dinner conversations at the Intermezzo Restaurant in Atlanta, where we had met weekly discussing the contents of this book as they unfolded. I would usually come armed with a half dozen books, showing new finds and new discoveries. Alex in return would frequently expound on the plight of the arts in the present time.

When I started reading Andre Breton's Surrealist Manifesto, I recognized the contents. Again, in our conversations at times Alex was repeating, almost word for word, lines from Andre Breton's Surrealist Manifesto. Then I realized, that he was again *remembering*. He had said it all before.

So, I began to study more about Breton. If the Surrealist Movement in art had a general—an organizer and commander—it was Andre Breton. He brought together artists, writers, poets. He defined their purpose, proposed what they should do. He gave them directions.

I marveled myself at my research, because as it unfolded it was as if I were being guided by an invisible hand. It often dramatically confirmed my projected scenarios, more dramatically than I would have anticipated. I was concluding that Andre Breton was not only the reincarnation of Arthur Rimbaud with all his fire and charisma, but that all this came down through the line stretching back to and including Alcibiades and Alexander the Great. Imagine Alcibiades with his flare and Alexander the Great with his charisma, and you have a picture of Andre Breton gathering his artists and writers around him. Breton would gather his "troops" in Paris at Certa or its annex Le Petit Grillon. At 25 he had become a formidable figure. He had a large head, thick wavy brown hair, blue eyes and a steel jaw. It was said that he had a combination of idealism and ruthlessness. It was said that he held his "disciples" enthralled.

When eating out, they would literally gather at his feet, and he would ask each what had they been doing with themselves as if they were to report. It was as though he had cast a spell over them. Today, we might call this kind of gathering a cult. Instead my study was suggesting that it was nothing more than the followers of Alexander the Great gathering around him his Royal Bodyguards and Royal Companions.

This Surrealist Movemement in art, over which Breton seemed to preside, included: Louis Aragon, Jean Arp, Luis Bunuel, Giorgio de Chirico, Salvador Dali, Robert Desnos, Marcel Duchamp, Paul Eluard, Max Ernest, Albert Giacometti, Rene Magritte, Andre Masson, Joan Miro, Benjamin Peret, Francis Picabia, Pablo Picasso, Jacques Prevert and his brother Pierre Prevert, Man Ray, Philippe Soupault, Yves Tanguy, Marie Toyen, Tristan Tzara, and others.

The first book I found on Surrealism (and that was its title) was by Patrick Waldberg. It conveniently had a Biographical Notes section in the back, with at least a paragraph descripton of each person in the Surrealist Movement, including birth and death dates. This enabled me to hasten my research, because I was still trying to fit each spirit into the chronological order of their succession of lifetimes. So, within seconds I could see that Andre Breton was born in 1896, 25 years after Rimbaud had died. Breton died in 1966, four years before Alex had been born. So, I considered that a fit.

Even before I began to look for my own lineage in this lifetime, I checked the death dates in the Biograhical Notes section, and found only two people there who would have died before I was born. They were Jacques Vache, a young man who died young, and who dramatically influenced Breton as his early friend. This did not seem to apply at all to the spiritual lineage of which I would have been a part. The only other person dying before I would have been born turned out to be a dramatic fit. He was Guilliaume Apollinaire. It was he who gave Surrealism its name, and its initial inspiration. It was Breton, who took the ball and ran with it. Apollinaire instinctively helped and supported every artist he could find. In the case of Chagall, he encouraged him and found an art gallery owner whom he encouraged to have Chagall's first exhibit.

As I looked back over my life, I, too had instinctively helped artists. In Baltimore, in the '60's, I had urged the dean of the College of Liberal Arts at the University of Baltimore to allow me to establish a film department modeled after the film department at the University of Southern California. I had then organized the Baltimore Experimental Film Society and encouraged literally every filmmaker I could find to make films and show them at showings I had organized. My goal was to provide them with a little income and an audience as an incentive to make more films. In arranging the showings of their films I was repeating the kind of encouragement Apollinaire had given to artists like Chagall. Among those young film-makers whose early films I encouraged and arranged showings for were John Waters and Steve Yeager, who won the First Place prize at Sundance for Best Documentary in 1998.

I had spent my time at the Daffodil Farm in the 1980's helping artists in their educational training, and encouraging them to get into the best art schools, and even arranging art shows for them, consistent with what Apollinaire had done in his lifetime.

Alex had accumulated a virtual library on alchemy, and at times, over the years when he began to speak of it, I knew he was remembering on a subconscious level his spiritual lineage, especially that of Rimbaud and Breton. He was always having grand and larger than life thoughts, when the topic would come up. And there was the usual wide-eyed smile. It always makes me happy, when I am aware that one of my former students and/or friends, has a consciousness that brings him to focus on his responsibilities far more than just for this one lifetime.

In 1994, when Alex informed me that he was going to go to Prague, I was happy for him and a little surprised. He had risen out of paying off student loans in his present job and had found a way to go to Europe. I always rejoice when anybody gets to go to Europe. Why Prague? He explained that it was the left bank of the 90's, and it was filled with students. These students were going to be the artists and leaders of the next generation. At that time I was immersed in programs at the farm, trying to help at-risk and emotionally and behaviorally disabled students. And as with all non-profit service organizations, I was trying to raise money to support the programs.

Prague seemed strange to me at that time. It was in Eastern Europe. Why would he want to go to Prague? Nonetheless, I was happy for him. He had a marvelous adventure in Prague, staying in a youth hostel on the side of the Vlatava River below the castle. Later he told me of a picnic in the orchard below the castle, where he and five other friends (after two bottles of wine each) had shed their clothes and frolicked. When he told me about leading the group of friends to shed their clothes, I thought of John Ridge leading his Cherokee classmates at the Moravian School in Chattanooga in the 1810's to shed their clothes at recess (to the horror of the missionary) and jump into Chickamauga Creek. I also thought of Alex, when he was 16, getting into trouble leading a number of male friends to streak down a quiet suburban neighborhood in the middle of the night in Iowa.

It would be six years before I would be able to go to Prague myself. Stories of Alex's trip had fascinated me. In the fall of 1999, I had become fascinated by a brief scene in a film I had seen, of a train arriving at a rural station somewhere in Europe. I had trouble explaining the fascination for the scene but somehow trusted my feelings, and found myself wanting to go there. I could not even discern the language on the railroad station, but began to look for similar place names in Europe, and found them on small towns in southeastern Germany, southern Poland, and the Czech Republic. I finally concluded they must be scenes around Prague.

I knew this is where I wanted to go. In one of the scenes from the film, I was surprised, after my research to realize, that I was looking at the Charles Bridge near the very site of Alex's youth hostel in Prague.

Once I got to Prague, Alex e-mailed me urging me to go to the orchard where he and his friends had frolicked naked, and lie on the grass, and feel the vibrations. I proceeded straight from the internet café at the foot of the Charles Bridge to the orchard beneath the castle, and lay down on the grass to feel the vibrations. I can't say that I felt the vibrations, but there were about a half dozen couples spread out throughout the orchard, in plain view, who probably could.

I was not in a position to consider going to Europe until I had exhausted all efforts to fund the programs at the farm and found it necessary to sell the farm to pay debts and get reestablished and begin Phase III. I had moved to Atlanta, which I had planned to use as a base of operation until I decided whether or not to live there. I was considering moving to L. A. (where I had a half dozen friends) or to Baltimore, where I also had some friends from the '60's. The next question was what was my next mission? Already the reading list as the bibliography for this book was the clear first item on my list of priorities. My reading of Plato's dialogues had also captured my imagination, and led me to view either staging or filming Plato's dialogues as going hand in hand with my writing a (this) book.

I had begun work on a screenplay for Plato's Dialogue ION, and concluded that it would be easier to find a European director interested in filming Plato, than an American one. On the internet I found a screenwriting class being offered in Prague, and I was on my way.

I arrived in Prague on July 1, 2000—good way to start the new millenium! I had been assigned a roommate in my dorm, and he turned out to be a film and video teacher from the U. S. and in my screenwriting class, so that could not have worked better.

One night he came in after a poetry reading and said, "You should go to the Café Slavia. I think you would enjoy it." I was not clear on why he thought I would enjoy it. But it was such a clear and direct suggestion, that I had long since begun to suspect that such as suggestion is not coming from the person making it, but is coming from a higher source. Either way, I decided to have lunch the next day at the Café Slavia. The restaurant was on the banks of the Vlatava River across the street from one of the state theatres, and with a clear view of Prague Castle. The ceilings were high, and the atmosphere was pleasant enough. I enjoyed it, but I was busy with the rest of my plans so I did not go back again, mostly because it was some distance from the dorm and the classroom building.

I had been in Prague for about two weeks before I began to discuss the contents of this book, since not everyone is broad minded enough to be able to talk about past lives. Many people still think New Age people are a little "far out" or "flaky," as I had just a few years before. But my readings had made me enthusiastic, if not passionate about my findings. After waiting for nearly a week to establish myself as a reasonable person, I finally mentioned to my roommate one night that I thought there was a chance I had been Guilliame Apollinaire in a previous lifetime. Instead of thinking I was crazy, he dealt with the new information with an open mind. I was relieved.

Two weeks later I ate breakfast at an English speaking American owned hotel near the dormitory and found information about an exhibit of art by a Czech artist, and it mentioned her friend Andre Breton. It was the first time I had realized Alex had been to Prague before, when he would have been Andre Breton. Not only that, but Andre Breton had fathered a child there. No wonder Alex had been so excited about Prague. He was walking over his faded footprints when he was Andre Breton. Then, I thought, "I wonder if he fathered the child in the orchard below the castle?"

One night my roommate arrived back in my room at nearly 3 a.m. from having been out on the town as our last days were drawing to a close. He excitedly told me how his instructor had given the students an assignment that day to write a screenplay about a place in Prague. Various sites were written on cards and placed in a hat. He had drawn the last card in the bottom of the hat, and it was Café Slavia. Later in the day, he had done his research and found that Guillaume Apollinaire was a regular customer there. Then we were both excited! I had not even known Apollinaire had been to Prague! I was walking over his faded footprints daily without knowing it. I had done that when I had eaten at the Café Slavia at the urging of my roommate weeks before. Obviously Apollinaire had walked all over Prague, perhaps even attended Charles University, as I had.

I told my roommate that I had lunch plans to eat in the cafeteria with a new friend, one of the students I had gotten to know, but that I would change our plans so we could meet instead at the Café Slavia. If we had been friends in a previous lifetime, we would be reuniting at our old haunt. My roommate had mentioned the book, *Magic Prague*, as having a whole chapter on Apollinaire. I decided I would spend the morning searching the bookstores of Prague looking for it. Once I found it, I would arrive early at the Café Slavia, find the section describing any regular friends of Apollinaire to see if they fit my new friend. We had met several times. He had traveled around the world, and had visited many countries over the past two years and was planning to write a book about his adventures. It occurred to me, that if I had been to Prague before, as Apollinaire, and had frequented the Café Slavia on a regular basis, then the new friend I had met in Prague, might be in my soul group. He might have been a constant companion of Apollinaire at the Café Slavia and be mentioned in *Magic Prague*.

It was cold and rainy, as most days had been that summer in Prague, and I was charging around the city streets. I had gone to three bookstores before I found a copy of *Magic Prague* at a bookstore behind the Tyn Church near the Old Town Square. I raced back to the Café Slavia, and while drinking several glasses of orange juice trying to warm up, I searched for my suspected friend. I found him right off. There was one constant companion of Apollinaire all right. He was called the "Wandering Jew," a name of mythical proportions, which was ascribed to a specific person who accompanied Apollinaire to the Café Slavia and seemingly everywhere throughout the enchanting city. Not only had I been walking over my faded footprints from a past lifetime, eating at one of my favorite and regular restaurants from that past lifetime, but I had found—rediscovered—an old friend.

After I returned from Prague, I found the brochure I had discovered that day at the American owned hotel, where I had had breakfast, learning that Andre Breton had been in Prague. It had information about an exhibit of a well known Prague artist, Toyen, at the House of the Stone Bell 11 May–6 August 2000. I had gone to see that exhibit. As I sat down to read over the brochure, while having breakfast one morning, I was astonished to turn the page and see a picture of Andre Breton, Toyen and Benjamin Peret seated side by side. The brochure said "For Toyen, Breton and Eluard's visit to Prague in 1935 was the beginning of inspiring personal relations."

The brochure described Toyen's activities. The occupation of Czechoslovakia by the Germans, however, radically interrupted her important international contacts and successes at home. Like other Surrealists, at the time, Toyen created her work illegally. Acting on a premonition of the Communist takeover, Toyen left Czechoslovakia in 1947 with the poet Jindrich Heisler. She settled in Paris, where she remained in exile until the end of her life. She took part in Surrealist activities at the side of Breton and Peret.

That morning in Prague, as if handed to me on a silver platter, here was information staring up at me alongside my scrambled eggs and sausages, telling me not only that Breton had been in Prague too, but the year he was in Prague—1935. In my research I had not run across information on Breton's visit to Prague. And perhaps Alex was with a future lifetime Toyen in his picnic in the orchard. And what about the other members of Alex's picnic? Had they been there before, too? And were they repeating an event they had been a part of before?

A year after my summer in Prague, and while preparing to write this chapter, I began looking for the brochure I've just mentioned among my files to remember the year that Breton would have been in Prague. I discovered something I had overlooked. He was in Prague not only with Toyen, but another member of the surrealist movement, Paul Eluard. That name jumped out at me, because in November after my summer in Prague, I had e-mailed my roommate. In his reply, he told me about one of the most interesting deams I've heard described. In it he makes reference to Apollinaire, who had returned from fighting in

World War I with a wound to his head which was bandaged. Here was his dream:

"As is common in your world, I had been thinking of you a lot of late. I had a dream in which I was making love on the Charles Bridge to a friend of mine from Paris, who for reasons only permissible in dreams (or David Lynch films) had grown her fingernails to an inordinate length—at least 12 inches. During our embrace-her being pinned against the wall of the bridge—she opened her mouth and her tongue unrolled to an unfathomable length as well, and started wrapping around my body. I looked over her shoulder and saw you in one of those silly paddleboats with a bandage on your head, a la Alpollinaire, smiling and making a U-turn on the Vltava. If that wasn't enough, a very handsome young boy, somewhat effiminate (one eye had dark make-up that was running a bit because for some reason it seems it had just started raining) and completely dressed in black (almost gothic like Johnny Depp in Edward Scissorhands), asked me for a light for his cigarette. Then, of course, the dream faded. I don't know what this means."

I wrote back to my former roommate and told him that was one of the best dreams I'd ever heard. But what had caught my attention was that his description evoked some poems by Paul Eluard, a member of the surrealist group. Here was my reply:

"If you were Paul Eluard, that means we would have known each other quite well in that lifetime, and both have been to Prague—though at different times, I think. At least, we both would have been familiar with all the sights—and roamed those streets before. (You may have done more 'roaming' than I.) I had thought as soon as I read your e-mail that dreams are often 'memories of the past.' This may mean that your dream was a memory from the past."

I had either forgotten, or it had not made an impression, certainly not a connection in my mind, that if my roommate were a reincarnation of Eluard, he would have been in Prague with Andre Breton in 1935! Andre Breton had been impressed with Apollinaire and inspired by him, so no doubt, he would have known about the Café Slavia which Apollinaire frequented so often. That he would have gone there with

Eluard, and perhaps regularly, would also have been likely. I would not be surprised if Eluard and Toyen as well would have been a part of any group which might have picnicked in the orchard, if in fact, Alex's picnic would have been a reliving of an event from his past as Breton.

LESSONS LEARNED—CHAPTER TEN

1. **Plan trips and vacations to better equip you for phases of your life mission.** The way I organized and spent the summer of 2000 was one of the best things I have ever done in my life. It included a four week study program in Prague: a two week class in screenwriting at Charles University and a two week class in journalism at the Prague Post, a week in Berlin, and more than two weeks in Oxford. It was designed to be a break between Phase 2 and Phase 3 of my life. I had gone with four possible objectives in mind, and had narrowed the focus to two by the end of the summer: (1) write this book, and (2) begin work on a screenplay for filming Plato's Dialogues. I would recommend that every person sit down and make an outline for your life—past and future.

2. **Divide your life into phases.** If you are in your teens or 20's, design a projected life plan. What would you like to do in your 20's, 30's, 40's, 50's. If you are in your 40's or 50's, design a plan for your '60's, '70', 80's, 90's. Remember, we are all supposed to be able to live to be 100, now, with the advances in medicine, if we take care of our bodies. In between phases, plan junctures, such as my summer in Europe, where I studied screenwriting and journalism. The internet is filled with descriptions of summer courses, internships, and jobs in places around the world. Plan events that will help you in accomplishing your life mission of making this a better world.

3. **Remember that the mind and spirit are better able to focus and function,** when some of the physiological aspects of your body are not so strong. A receptionist in a business office, while I was waiting for an appointment once said, "I was nothing but raging hormones until I turned 50, and then I began to live." She recommend a book, entitled, *Age Wave* by Ken Dychtwald, which describes the advantages of getting older.

4. **Consciously think about and look for clues to past lives.** I learned, once I got to Prague, that I had been there in a past life, and was walking over my own "faded footprints." The value of searching for and discovering our past lives is that it gives meaning and depth to our present lives, and points a direction for the future. We should ask, "If I spent time in this place in the past, how does it help me in this lifetime? If I am not using what I learned then in what I am doing now, then how can I learn better how to do it?"

5. **Be alert to those around you as supplying important information.** Someone like my roommate in Prague was an incredibly important channel of information for me. Without him I would not have known that Apollinaire had been there or the significance of the Café Slavia. Be open to every person you meet. They may be a channel of information for you, filled with messages or instructions that could change your life. I am tempted to start a conversation with everyone I sit next to at a counter in a restaurant, in case this is someone who has a message. Sometimes when I don't start a conversation I wonder if I might have missed a major opportunity for a contact, potential friend or message that that person may have had for me. Sometimes I'll start a conversation just to be sure. After a few sentences it may be sufficiently clear that this is not the case.

11

Seeing in the Dark: Imagine human beings living in an underground cavelike dwelling.

In *The Republic,* Plato asks us to imagine human beings living in a cave-like dwelling. Then he asked us to imagine that they've been there since childhood with light coming from a fire burning behind them. He says they are like us, in that they see nothing of themselves and those around them, only their shadows. How could they if they keep their heads motionless facing the wall in front of them? Then the prisoners would believe there is nothing of the truth except the shadows they see in front of them. If freed, the prisoners would have been so accustomed to seeing only the shadows that they would be virtually blinded by the light, and unable to recognize the truth, since they had believed for so long that the shadows in front of them was reality.

These passages from Plato's dialogue *The Republic*, present the best known images from all his works—the analogy of the cave. This is an extremely important first step in *seeing in the dark*. Virtually everything we see and accept as reality is not. It is but a shadow pointing to a reality beyond what we see, feel and experience. Our first challenge is to not see the physical body when we look at another person. What we are looking at is a container of the spirit, locked into that body.

If we see a person as a "black" person, or an "old" person, or a "gay person", then obviously we are NOT seeing that person. We are seeing the temporary current lifetime container of the person's soul and not even beginning to see his or her personality much less his or her divine eternal spirit. We are seeing their mask, their costume, their uniform, but not the real person underneath. They may be "wearing" it for a specific mission or to learn a specific lesson in this lifetime.

Over the years I developed various names for the body a person occupies during a lifetime. Those names include: container, shell, puppet (with the spirit inside being the puppeteer—pulling the strings), tin can. My favorite concept is a World War II tank. This came to me one night as I was sitting at a bar looking across at the people on the other side. It was as though I were looking out of these little slits (like you see in World War II movies, such as "Saving Private Ryan.") We use the eyes to function like the periscope in a submarine, which, of course, becomes yet another analogy for the body.

Then, of course, it is Socrates who perhaps describes it best. In Plato's Dialogue *Phaedo*, Socrates says that we mortals are in a sort of prison, and that a man must not, apparently, free himself from it, or try to run away."

IDEAS ARE LIKE SURGICAL IMPLANTS PLACED INTO THE MIND.

Ideas are "placed" into our heads. Dr. Brian Weiss speaks of Master Spirits speaking to and through us. Whether they or spirit guides, also called guardian angels, do it, it happens as clearly as if a brain surgeon placed them there. We are not knowledgeable of this spiritual activity, since it is happening in a spiritual dimension, which we cannot see and do not understand (any more than people understood astronomy 2,000 years ago). When an idea "pops" into our heads, we think how great we are for "having thought of that." We assume credit for all sorts of mental ingenuity, not out of arrogance, but out of ignorance.

We are being guided and led in almost everything we do, with a spiritual "supervisor" to use a common workplace analogy. We are also being led with uncanny synchronization in the course our lives are intended to follow.

For example, when I started assembling a group of people in Atlanta for a reading of the screenplay on Plato's dialogues, I realized we could achieve three things at once. We would (1) discuss the screenplay, (2) discuss the possibility of presenting it as a play in addition to filming it, and (3) simply have a philosophical discussion of the ideas in Plato's dialogues.

Continuing along this line of thinking, I said to myself, "Now what could we name this group? Should we call it a "committee" (too formal an organization), or should we simply call it a "group" (too informal). While I was still pondering this concept, I began research on Florence for the next chapter I was writing, and as I turned the page, there was the answer.

It was as if the name had been handed to me on a silver platter. The group that was forming in my mind, and in reality, was a—reactivating, reliving—of Cosimo de Medici's "Platonic Academy." I was acting out in a new setting the function Marsilio Facino served during that lifetime. Suddenly I realized several things were happening at once. (1) Ideas were being *placed* into my mind as though with a surgeon's scalpel, except that in this case the surgeon was a Master Spirit. (2) I was repeating, in this lifetime, what I had done in the lifetime of Marsilio Facino. I was not just repeating but redefining—refining—translating the same essential message of Plato's Dialogues to my generation in its own language (film), the same way Facino had done in his generation (from Greek to Latin). (3) And now I was REMEMBERING what I had done before.

Becoming aware that this kind of process is happening for each and everyone one of us is a way in which we can see beyond the shadows to the fire that casts them. We are continually acting in concert with other members of our soul group refining—redefining—interpreting our message or lifetime purpose in this time and place. Being conscious that this is happening every day will help us see and come to understand the spiritual reality and presence that is guiding our lives.

THE WORLD OF IDEAS.

For several years during the '80's, Joseph Campbell was a star. Campbell was a sociology professor who moderated a television series entitled: *The Power of Myth*. The program was mentally stimulating and exciting. His survey of principles, practices, and behavior patterns of societies around the world was visually entertaining. It was seeing the world pre-Travel Channel, except that we had a college professor rather than entertaining tour guides leading us. We were also being presented lectures on the history of sociology.

The presentation of these ideas about primitive societies stimulated the mind the way a college or professional football game might stimulate the senses. We were seeing the world as one cohesive story: how primitive societies evolved into more sophisticated ones. We learned how societies had patterns of behavior for a reason.

IDEAS ARE THE FOOD OF THE SPIRIT.

Not only are *ideas* food for the nourishment of the mind (the muscles of the mind are in the physiology of the brain), they are, of course, food for the spirit as well. Ideas are *given* to the mind from a *spiritual realm*. We are being *fed* with ideas, as though it were fruit, which come from *the realm of Master Spirits*. According to Aldous Huxley in his book, *The Doors of Perception*, by definition for the intellectual, using Goethe's phrase, the "word" is essentially "fruitful" or like fruit. He sees the urge to "transcend" self-consciousness as being the main appetite of the soul. If this is true, then ideas are vehicles that get us into the Spiritual Realm. Like food gives the body strength and energy to walk, work and play, *ideas* give our minds and spirits food to "transcend" *self*-consciousness. Another way to say it is that ideas are spiritual foods, which provide the key and roadmap for enabling us to transcend the physical and enter into the Spiritual Realm.

It is a truism to point out how addiction to television and movies (as opposed to reading) limits the imagination. But it is a problem when we realize that everything is thought over for us and delivered already digested by "the boob tube." More and more movies are made that don't deal with ideas at all. Car chases replace the horse chases in the Saturday western at the movies. The good guy still chases after the bad guy. Murder and violence, all bypass ideas and head straight for the emotions. One can watch an entire movie and hardly have his mind stimulated at all. These are cheap thrills, and provide virtually no "food for the soul." The danger is we lose our "mental muscle," and any desire to transcend our physical bodies which are on an escalator, which, at a steady and constant speed, is carrying each one of us to an inevitable death.

Many people try to transcend this inevitability by going to church every Sunday. Huxley speaks of "the mild sense of virtue" which the average Sunday churchgoer gains from "ninety minutes of boredom." Do we really think those 90 minutes of weekly church going attendance is somehow going to lift us off the escalator and spare us?

PAST AND FUTURE LIFETIMES.

I had always thought of belief in past and future lifetimes as something that was a part of Eastern thought—the religions of Hinduism, Buddhism and Confucianism. Dr. Brian Weiss researched the topic and found that it was a part of Judaism and the early Christian belief system until the Emperor Constantine decided to use Christianity as a state religion. This solidified his country under one state religion rather than having a large number of bickering and competing ones. If Christians continued to believe that once we die our spirit automatically and instantly moves out of our bodies into a state of bliss waiting to enter our next, new body, then the state would have no power over that person. Death would merely be a passageway from one life to the next. Fear of death would no longer exist. So, this belief in past and future lifetimes was removed from the early Christian belief system. I attended a lecture by Brian Weiss at the Jewish Community Center (when it was on Peachtree Street) in Atlanta. He said that it was also part of the early Jewish beliefs, and the strength of the belief in past and future lifetimes faded with the industrial revolution, in which the emphasis shifted from a spiritual/mystical approach to understanding the world to a scientific one.

In Plato's Dialogue *Phaedo* Socrates says that a man will be born and will die again several times over—a soul being so strong it survives several births. In Plato's Dialogue *Meno* Socrates describes the soul as being something that dies but is born again, being something that is immortal and never destroyed. Therefore, he concludes that a man ought to live in perfect holiness. He speaks of a soul as having seen all things that exist and having knowledge of them. He proposes that man knows more than he could possible know out of one lifetime, but that learning is "recollection."

This is profound, of course, and shows us how little we have learned, since our contemporary efforts toward "learning" is to fill a person's mind with outward facts and information, and train him in a trade skill. All of this is outward knowledge imposed on the individual from *without*. Socrates is saying here, that all learning is *within*. If we can *remember*, from our pasts (past lives), then we have the ability to truly learn. This book is intended to be a first step in providing us with some tools to help us *remember*.

Socrates speaks of the Master Spirits as "gods," or to use the term of the New Age writers "spirit guides." These spirit entities are most frequently referred to in the Christian context as "guardian angels." Whether we use the classical Greek term of gods, or the New Age term of spirit guides, or the Christian term of guardian angels, we are speaking of the same relationship between our physical mortal bodies which house an immortal soul and its relationship with the divine.

Socrates speaks of our having a knowledge, acquired before birth, which we lost while being born. By applying the senses to things in question, he proposes we regain that knowledge which we formerly possessed. Then he says "learning" will be the recovery of the knowledge which is our own.

The purpose of this book is to help us find this "lost knowledge"—we lost it while being born. It may be that the vast storehouse of knowledge we have repressed would simply be too much for a soul to grasp in a small child's body in a new lifetime. If we are alert and questioning, as we grow "in knowledge and love," then we begin to meet up with our soul group, and learn about our past lives and resources we gained then, and how to use them now.

PEOPLE AS MESSENGERS.

My favorite movie scene, depicting the way in which the Master Spirits speak to us, is in the film made for television of *The Odyssey*, in 1997, in which Isabella Rossellini plays the part of the Greek Goddess Athena. She is the household goddess of the family of Odysseus. When Odysseus is returning from Troy, and his house is full of men wanting to marry his wife in order to gain ownership of his house and lands, his son Telemachus played by Alan Stenson is in a fit of despair (quite understandably). Fearing his father has perished in the long journey home, Telemachus, in one scene, is being encouraged by an old household servant not to despair, but to have hope. Telemachus pays no attention to the old man, and leaving him behind, storms up the rocky beach.

Suddenly, a rock by itself hurls up from the beach and strikes Telemachus in the forehead knocking him down. The old man's words of encouragement turn to laughter, but his laughter is not that of an old man but a that of a woman, and we see that the old man is not an old man at all, but we are miraculously beholding Athena standing where old man's body was.

The goddess Athena then speaks directly and visibly to the young Telemachus. She reassures him that his father is all right, and that he will return, and that Telemachus must have hope and faith that he will.

In exactly this way, Spirits who are watching over us and protecting us are speaking to us all the time. It may be through an old man or servant, as in the case of Telemachus. Or it may be through the body and voice of a teacher, friend, parent, brother, sister, spouse, son, daughter, employer, employee or a stranger on the street, in a bar or in the subway. We must be alert to every person we meet or encounter. That person may be the carrier of the next message from a Master Spirit.

Recently, I was seated at a bar counter of a restaurant in Atlanta having just completed my dinner, and suddenly a man sat down two seats away, but on a side of the counter, so that we were at a 90 degree angle, and he seemed to be directly facing me. So, unusual was this, that rather than leave, as I was ready to, I ordered an additional cup of coffee. Three times I attempted to start a conversation giving him full opportunity to deliver a message (if he were there to do so). By the third try, I concluded that this was not the case, so after paying my bill and without finishing my coffee I left.

The ways to look for messages being delivered are:

1. When the person is unusually insistent on advising you to do something.

2. When the nature of the quote or message is highly unusual or even contradictory for the person making the statement.

3. When the message is unusually appropriate for your situation, word for word, what you need to hear in that time and place.

The best thing to do is try to analyze everything somebody says or does. I don't mean to wear yourself out doing this, or working at it, but just being alert to the fact that at that moment that person may be a "divine messenger." Two excellent examples of this occurred in Prague in 2000. Before I left the United States, a friend insisted I go to Berlin in order to see two museums: The Pergamon Museum and the Egyptian Museum. Several times when I saw her before leaving she insisted strongly that I make a point to see these museums. Even after I got to Europe, and was in Prague, she e-mailed me to insist that I go.

This certainly met the criteria above, and I knew by the time I got the e-mail in Prague, that this was not the friend talking. This was the guidance if not the insistence of a Master Spirit. I shifted my thinking, once I realized this, and it became more of an order, command or instruction. When I arrived in Berlin, seeing those museums became my number one priority. At the Pergamon Museum, when I discovered that the statue of Athena had been moved, I spent a second day looking for the museum, to which it had been moved. I spent the following day looking for the Egyptian museum.

In all of these Museum searches, I felt clearly guided and directed there by a Master Spirit who was speaking *insistently* through my friend. It turned out to be almost like a classroom lesson on my spirit's past. In the case of the Egyptian Museum, I found the famous sculpted head of Nefertiti in existence. It was a mold used by royal sculptors in Egypt, to make official copies which were spread throughout the city. It is the one picture of Nefertiti in virtually all the history books on this period of Egyptian history. This explained why one eye seems to be unfinished. I realized that Nefetiti was a part of one of the Royal Families in Egypt, of which I was a part in an earlier lifetime. I looked for a genealogical chart, and, again, as though I were being led, there it was on the wall in the next room, exactly where I went looking for it, and I saw the connection. I realized then that this was part of "my" spiritual past—"my" spiritual lineage.

At the Pergamon Museum, as well as the museum where I eventually found the statue of Athena that originally stood in the entrance to the library at Pergamon, I felt again, that I was looking at something I had seen and experienced before.

A few years before I discovered that Galen had been born and grew up in Pergamon and would have gone past the Great Altar to study in the library, and before I concluded that I would be in *his* spiritual lineage, I wrote these words: "For whatever reason, I still find the Great Altar at Pergamon to be one of the most beautiful buildings architecturally I have ever see. The passion I feel for the beauty of this building is not an accident. I believe it is explainable. I believe I beheld its beauty in a previous lifetime. I believe that *I remember.*"

12

Making the Invisible Visible

C. S. Lewis, in *The Magician's Nephew* in *The Chronicles of Narnia* del-cares that we have come from another world—by magic! Often the language of science fiction or the symbolism of children's stories, such as *The Chronicles of Narnia* and the Harry Potter books, are free to carry expressions of the language of the mysterious. It goes beyond what our limited "adult" practical minds can comprehend to describe images and metaphors from another dimension.

The evidence of all the research on near death experiences, and those thousands by now who have, through hypnosis, been able to explore events in their past lives, indicates that a spirit we cannot see inhabits our very physical mortal body with all its limitations. The process of a spirit (soul) entering a tangible and physical body seems preposterous, and yet our religions tell us it is so. Children's books refer to it as "magic", and philosophers say our souls are imprisoned in these bodies, and, on death, they will be free.

DEATH IS JUST ANOTHER OUT OF BODY EXPERIENCE.

One of the things I'm proposing in this book about our understanding of history, psychology's development of personality and the immortality of the soul is that it brings us to an understanding of death from a new perspective. From hundreds and now thousands of documented near death experiences that people have recorded, we hear them tell how they left their bodies and hovered in the sky or near the ceiling looking down on their bodies. Their spirits clearly "went out of" their bodies. Some accounts tell of conversations with a Master Spirit in which they discussed whether their "job...their mission" in this lifetime had been completed. If not, they returned to their bodies and fought for their lives if they had been in an accident or were extremely ill. According to New Age writers, if their mission here is complete, they go to a place filled with love where they meet with members of their soul group. Descriptions of that place in accounts of New Age writers and from preachers of the funeral sermons of my aunts and uncles I heard as a child in north Georgia, are virtually identical. Perhaps it takes a child to understand and see, as the child did in *Finding Neverland,* that death is an adventure. I am fond of saying, "Death is like taking a nap, and then waking up in a new body." While conveying an overview, that description does not take into account the important time between lives, of gathering and planning for the next future lifetime. Nor does it account for my mother's nurses, seeing her standing just behind the minister as he preacher her funeral sermon, nor the conversation I had with my brother in a dream a year and half after he died.

REMEMBER THE BODY IS JUST A MACHINE— LIKE A CAR THAT GETS US WHERE WE'RE GOING.

Remember the body is just a machine, and a temporary one at that. It's good for our mission in this life, and that's it. It amuses me how much emphasis people, especially young people, place on youth, or the way our machine looks for a few years. Most of us are born with a spirit 3,000 years old. What difference is a mere 60 or 70 more years going to make? The phrase "Wise for his age" or "Wise for his years" simply means that person they're describing *is remembering* early in this lifetime. I'm fond of saying "I'm 14 in an aging body." What I mean by that is that I remain filled with the excitement and sense of adventure one has (at 14) with his life ahead of him. I'm excited about the adventures remaining in this lifetime, and I'm already talking with my soul group members, anticipating our time in between lifetimes, about where we might spend our next lifetime. I'm fascinated with scenes of Hong Kong, though Berlin is more likely going to get my vote, if I have one.

WE HAVE CHOSEN OUR BODIES FOR A REASON.

We are in our present bodies for a reason. We can't all be Olympic athletes, or beautiful Hollywood starlets, born of wealthy parents and never having to worry about money, or dashingly handsome. If we are, that's for a reason. If we are not, that is for a reason. If we choose our parents, as New Age writers say, that is to facilitate us in accomplishing our individual and group missions. Our bodies may be the simple genetic result of that, or they may facilitate our personality traits coming down from one lifetime to the next. At the very least, we may be here to learn and grow, and our present bodies facilitate that. Our present lifetime here is a temporary journey, and as Socrates might have asked Ion at the end of the dialogue carrying Ion's name: Do you want to be just another mortal body that will die, or do you want to be divine?

I think if we realized what the stakes are, most of us would answer, divine. For all of us can be Messengers of God—carrying His love throughout each day in our hearts, and expressing it in our every act toward others.

All of the time we are surrounded by things that we cannot see. I don't just mean spiritual entities or parallel dimensions, which people without imagination scoff at behind the smokescreen: "You can't prove it." I am referring to scientific "facts."

MAKING THE INVISIBLE VISIBLE.

Scientists are enabling us to "see in the dark" all the time. At least weekly, and at times daily, we read about scientists making yet another breakthrough in astronomy, archaeology and medicine. Telescopes are scanning the skies all the time searching for new planets or asteroids within our own solar system and others. We cannot see, with our naked eye, all the planets in our solar system, but we *believe* that they are there. We *believe* the scientists who have enabled us to "see in the dark." Then there are microscopic "entities" crawling around on our skin and in our bodies we cannot see. When we have a rash, our doctor may have to take a scraping and then examine it under a microscope in order to "see" what kind of microscopic parasite may be causing the rash.

We, as children, have all been confined to home with an illness. As the strong rays of light streamed through the window on a bright sun lit afternoon, I remember being shocked to see the thousands of tiny dust particles that filled the space between my eyes and the window—particles which we are *breathing*! So, the empty space, between us and the window, is not empty at all, but it is filled with tiny particles of dust.

Scientists, then, are among the first to enable us *to see in the dark*. Through their telescopes we are able to see millions of miles into space. We can study the history and origins or our universe. We can study the history of life forms that inhabited our planet before us. We can study the mineral content of our planet.

In addition to these scientific "seers," there are artists who, using Anton Chekhov's definition of art, are continually involved in the "search for the truth and the meaning of life." In the simplest form, these artists hold up mirrors, so that we can see through their paintings, sculpture, plays in the theatre, films, and photography the horror, absurdity, beauty, and wonder of life. When we have a mirror held up to ourselves—to our weaknesses, strengths, sadness, and glories—then the artist acts as a visionary. He, like the scientist, is a seer. He helps us see the human drama in full emotional and personal terms, which often the scientist does not or cannot do. We are confronted by art whereas science just informs. Art often challenges us to act—to respond. In this way artists are "messengers of God." Artists are often called to their work—like Van Gogh, who painted because he had to, not because he was doing it to make a lot of money.

MESSENGERS ARE SURROUNDING US ALL THE TIME.

These scientists and artists are visible, tangible *messengers*—in their professions and daily roles—taking off the cloaks of ignorance, which cover the truth. They at least, in part, allow us to look at the light from the shadows—to use Plato's analogy of the cave. But take note that this "truth" is migratory. New planets, solar systems, black holes are constantly being discovered. New diseases, new drugs, new cures are always being discovered. Archaeologists and anthropologists are always discovering new human species and settlements. We are living in an expanding world of knowledge in every science.

But while we are reaching outward to know more about the world, we are constantly making more visible and accessible spirit entities, which are reaching invisibly toward us, patiently ready to lead and guide us if we will but allow them.

They make themselves known by:

1. **Coincidences.** Coincidences are virtually the voice of the spirit world, letting us know we are not alone. A coincidence is a call to wake up, pay attention, know that what is happening, or what is going to happen, has meaning. It is an intrusion through the "door in the wall" into our physical world by a Master Spirit. It may also be a reassurance that we are doing the right thing—that we are *on course*.

2. **People entering and leaving our lives.** Some relationships don't last an entire lifetime. We may have friends who only last a certain number of years. They have entered our lives for a purpose. We need to understand that purpose and take advantage of it.

3. **People are messengers, channels, through which divine messages come to us.** It is very much like we are living in a science fiction movie. A spirit steps into the body of someone we know, or some stranger at the bar. Without being aware that he is being used in

this way, a friend or stranger may say what comes into his head. What comes into his head is natural to him. But it may seem to us as though it is a carefully, almost surgically, "implanted" idea by a Master Spirit seeking to communicate with us. **It is.** The orchestration of events in his life may have produced events and fashioned his thinking at that very moment in time, to perfectly produce the message that he needs to receive at that point. The old servant of the family in the "The Odyssey," who becomes transformed so that we see Athena standing in his place, is such an example. Athena *was* standing in his body delivering the message that Telamachus heard in the voice of the old man.

We are living in a **MESSAGES BEING SENT** world. Once we become conscious of this fact, it will seem like someone has turned on the light. Suddenly we will realize messages have been coming to us all the time, and we have been unaware of them. We need to be **TUNED IN** and **TURNED ON** all the time.

HOW TO SEE IN A "PRACTICAL" WORLD.

The problem with living in an age of practicality, in an age of materialism, is that we no longer allow ourselves to believe in the mysterious. We falsely believe that everything is explainable. Sometimes one must become impractical in order to be able to enter the "door in the wall." Often, it takes a disaster or an accident or the loss of a loved one or an illness to remove us from the monotony of day to day existence. It often takes a crisis to enable us to see into the world of the spirit.

When I had concluded the arts program at the farm in 1989, I had paid all my expenses that fall, following the income from the summer program. It was the best year financially, that we had ever had. But I realized suddenly, and overwhelmingly, that I could never recover from debt incurred with that program. In short, that program had to end. I could not go on. It was the first time I had come to that realization in ten years.

I felt as if some giant hand had wrapped itself around my feet, and I was lifted into the air and thrown onto my back on the floor. I was in the den, and I remember that image very vividly. That was it. The program was finished. Nothing less dramatic would have changed the direction in which I was head, and it was (in retrospect) important to make that change. It was a lesson that I was supposed to learn, and a sentence formed in my mind at that moment that I have never forgotten. That sentence was: "You can see God better when you are flat on your back."

LEARNING TO STAND IN YOUR BEAM.

If each of us does have 80 or more lifetimes, and we are here with a purpose or mission, then our whole view of our world, and ourselves in it, changes.

I refer to this purpose filled life as "standing in your beam." The understanding of a beam of light emanating from God, is not only a good analogy, but it is the exact picture of what people see during near death and out-of-body experiences. The person's spirit floats toward the top of the room or outside area, and he or she is looking down on his or her body. From the body upward is a beam of light, at the upper end of which is a light as bright as the sun, which emanates pure love. This funnel and beam of light has been drawn by more than one artist.

OUT OF THIS WORLD.

Is there life beyond the physical world we see and experience? There are those who have died who have come back to tell us. The pioneer researcher in the field of Near Death Experiences (those who have clinically died, but been resuscitated and recounted what they saw and heard while clinically dead) and the inclusive out of body experience, is Dr. Raymond Moody. In his book *Life After Life*, he relates how he became interested.

While an undergraduate student studying philosophy at the University of Virginia, he learned about a case of someone clinically dead, who had been revived and given an account of what had happened. He had filed the experience away.

Later he tells of teaching at a university in Eastern North Carolina. He was teaching from Plato's Dialogue *Phaedo* on the subject of immortality. After class one of his students stopped by to tell him about his grandmother's having clinically died, but being revived, and afterwards she recounted a view of what she had experienced almost identical to the description Dr. Moody had heard at the University of Virgina.

In Dr. Moody's book, which is a study of more than 100 people who have been declared 'clinically' dead, but who have been revived, there are common descriptions of life after death. Thus, we have witnesses who have been there, and tell us their eye-witness accounts of what each of us faces after we pass out of this body.

GOD'S THUNDERBOLTS HURLED THROUGH TIME.

It is very important for us to learn to think vertically. By that I mean that we must come to see ourselves in a time line in history. Not only is it important to study World History and American History, but we should learn the history of the city, county and region where we live. We will never know if we are walking on our own faded footprints if we are ignorant of the history of the place where we live. I once read that during the Civil War General William Sherman was nearly killed by the explosion of a shell near where he was riding just north of Adairsville, Georgia on May 17, 1864 during his march through Georgia from Dalton to Atlanta. Had he been killed, the war may have been prolonged. It certainly would have been different.

I decided to explore where this would have been. There were three Northern Armies separating south of Resaca, Georgia, and the one which Sherman himself led went down the Old Tennessee Road between Calhoun and Adairsville. I then researched where that Old Tennessee Road would have been, and discovered to my surprise that Interstate 75 was constructed literally over the top of it. As one heads north on Interstate 75 from Georgia Highway 140, or the Adairsville exit, the driver can see the Old Tennessee Road appearing first on the right, then is lost by the Interstate having been built over it, until it reappears on the left, then it turns back and disappears again. Some old houses that stood during the Civil War are still there alongside the interstate highway. I had driven down this stretch of Interstate 75 many, many times over the years, and had never noticed the old road, nor known of this history.

Tens of thousands of tourists drive this way every year without any idea that they are driving past this history. How much it would illuminate our lives, if we but knew the history of our own hometowns, and locations where we work everyday. But more important, it gives us a sense of distance in time from the past to the present day.

Every person should be required to study genealogy. It starts with your personal history, and shows how you are connected to all previous times. Understanding one's family structure also gives the basic family unit, as a basis for understanding the soul group in spiritual lineaging. It is difficult to know your favorite period of history if you are unfamiliar or uneducated in what happened during the various periods of history.

THE ART OF BEING POROUS.

Once we begin to be *conscious* that we are living in a world where we are only seeing shadows, (to use Plato's analogy in *The Republic*) and that behind the world we think we see there is a spiritual reality or world illuminating everything and causing the shadows to be cast, then we can begin to turn around to see the light.

That light emanates from God, and it is a pure stream of love. This is what people feel when they leave the confines of their physical bodies when they have near-death experiences. We need to realize that the Master Spirits are speaking to us all of the time. They speak to us through other people, and they may use us and speak and act in us to others as well. As we become conscious of this, our consciousness will expand to and through two levels. The first level is *seeing beauty*, and the second level *experiencing love*. This will affect our thinking and living in two ways: (1) We will begin to see the beauty in *all things*, and (2) seeing that beauty automatically will lead to love—*love of all people and all things*. These are the two levels of consciousness which we need to grow to and through.

My reading journey began with a television series on astronomy. Some time after seeing it, I discovered a book in the library of incredibly beautiful photographs of the universe. I remember turning to one specific photograph of a galaxy. The heavens were ablaze in color and forms. I remembering being overwhelmed by its beauty, but what was more remarkable, I remember that that beauty literally drew love out of me like a magnet, and I sat there not only awed with beauty but bathed in love, which seemed to come to and then through me.

As we expand our consciousness and move through the phases, we will increasingly become porous, and the love of God will pour through us and out to others and out into the world.

HOW POROUS LIVES EXPRESS THE PRESENCE OF GOD.

In his book, *Many Lives, Many Masters*, Dr. Brian Weiss says that our purpose is to grow in knowledge and love. Much of my reading on my reading journey was done at the Daffodil Farm. I was doing much of my research at the Rome, Georgia library and afterwards eating dinner at a restaurant nearby. In the library I was literally pouring through books, almost feeling my mind expand with knowledge. It was a tangibly exciting process. What I found happening, was that as I was gaining knowledge, I was simultaneously and without doing anything else to encourage it, growing it love. I would go from the library to the restaurant, where I would frequently eat at the counter. I would be facing farmers, young college students talking about "chicks" and their romantic exploits, tired businessmen after a hard day at the office and construction workers.

After my day at the library, having filled my mind with new information about history, the universe, philosophy, architecture and art, I realized I was having this overwhelming feeling that *love* was pouring out of me across the counter to those people on the other side. Without explanation and without expecting it, I felt love for all those people—mostly total strangers.

My gaining knowledge had resulted in my automatically gaining love. I have often wondered if the reverse is not also true. That ignorance and lack of knowledge results in hate.

Not only, then, should we be porous and allow God's love to enter and go through us out into the world, but we should work toward this consciously. I think of myself and others as being like a "finger" of God: the way blood flows into a finger and returns to the heart, and circulates again. God's love should flow through us in a like manner, and then as it returns to God, it will circulate through us again. We can thus come to see ourselves as fingers on the hands of God, doing His will in the world.

LIVING IN THE HEARTS AND MINDS OF OTHERS.

Once we move through the level of seeing beauty in all things, and consequently become instruments of God's love, then we live in a friendly universe. We are sharing space and time on this planet during our lifetimes with other people as well as animals and plants. We cohabit the planet with them. The Native Americans understood this. They apologized to animals for having to kill them for food. They saw the trees and the forests as brothers and sisters. They saw the beauty in all things.

LEARNING TO DISAPPEAR.

When we become aware that we are but a "finger of God," and have achieved the goal of being porous, then when we meet and talk with a person, even during the conversation, we will have an unspoken message in our hearts. We will be thinking: "This person standing in front of me is absolutely beautiful." Concentrate on the extreme beauty of the inner person you are looking at. That person is unique in all the world. There has never been, there is not now on the planet earth, nor will there ever be in all future history a person anything like this person you are looking at. Marvel in that uniqueness.

Concentrate on disappearing, so that your body becomes a disappearing shell, and in its place is pure knowledge—pure love. God stands where your body was, exploding in love toward that person. You will feel the glow and the power of that thought, and so will the other person. If you are focusing and concentrating on loving the person in front of you with all your heart and mind, wait for his recognition. You will see it, when it comes to him, by the expression on his face. Then you will be between a smile and laughter, and so will the person in front of you.

THE KNOWLEDGE CONSPIRACY.

This then, needs to be the quest of a new generation. We need to know that there is more to life than television, computers, money and greed. This generation has not yet learned that they *can* find the answers, but they have to search for them. This is not a new search, but one which has occupied every generation. It is a search for the meaning of life. When each person enters into the new world of beauty and love, fulfilling his life with a goal-directed mission, working with his soul group reliving-refining-redefining to a new generation that ongoing life purpose, then each person will know his place in the time line of history. Like a lightning bolt hurled down through time, like a streaking comet across the sky, he will illuminate everyone he meets in all his endeavors. As he moves about each day, he will greet each person he meets with a subtle smile and a message in his heart which will say, "I know."

Epilogue

The writing of this book began in the late 1990's and was completed in its present form in 2001. It was updated and revised in 2006, but the expansion of knowledge, and consciousness that it records, continues. One of the most encouraging and affirming things about it is the circle of friends around me, who not only comprise my soul group, but they have become enthusiastic participants in the ongoing search for and expansion of this spiritual lineage knowledge. One friend, a former student, who is now an architect, organized two trips to Nashville to see the only reconstructed replica of the Parthenon in the world. On these trips we discussed the Greek lifetime in Athens, of course, but also the Cherokee lifetime which is why we are both in Georgia, where the Cherokee history would have taken place. It soon became obvious to me, that he would have been Leonard Hicks, son of Chief Charles Hicks. Leonard Hicks and Elias Boudinot would have made a trip to Cornwall, Connecticut, when they were 14, and had remained friends since. Leonard came back on a ship from that school with Cherokee Chief Major Ridge, and they sailed into Charleston. I explain my friend's love and recurring trips to Charleston from Atlanta as having their origins with his trip in his Cherokee lifetime.

When I told another friend about our Surrealist artist lifetime in Paris, he brought a copy of Smithsonian Magazine with a an article about Modigliani and, pointing to his picture, said, "This is who I was in the Surrealist lifetime." At first I didn't know whether he was joking or not, but when I brought him a DVD on the life of Modigiliani, he gave it to his mother to look at, obviously being serious all along.

After initially joking with a female friend about being the nagging wife of Cicero, Terentia, in a previous lifetime, she as well as my other friends picked up on the label, and the reference has stuck. Once a friend, visiting from California, sent me an e-mail saying he wanted to be sure to meet Terentia. His computer's word check changed the spelling to torrential. So, we had fun calling my friend "torrential." She takes her Roman lifetime seriously, and to my surprise read a history of Cicero and pointed out some of my friends in this lifetime's soul group as being children of Cicero and Terentia in that lifetime.

I had my first serious conversation with another friend, shortly after he was graduated from college. His mother had told me that, at 12, he said he was going to write the great American novel. After I had spoken to him in our first conversation, I told him he had been Aristophanes in our classical Greece lifetime. Aristophanes was present at Plato's Dialogue *Symposium* with Socrates and Alcibiades. This friend, after rejecting pressures to conform to traditional occupations, is pursuing his writing full time. In my last phone conversation with him, he was telling me he is now reading the complete plays of Aristophanes.

Not all of my friends accept the concept of past lives. One of those mostly clearly would have been David Brown in the Cherokee lifetime. David Brown was a writer about the Cherokee country, and he lived at New Echota. He went to the Moravian Mission school in Cornwall, Connecticut along with Leonard Hicks and Elias Boudinot, and then to Andover Theological Seminary in Newton, Massachusetts. Whether accepting it or not, my present friend is walking over the faded footprints of David Brown. Not only did he make a memorial visit to the farm, the birthplace and childhood home of Elias Boudinot, but he has moved from Atlanta and now lives in Newton, Massachusetts where the seminary that David Brown attended in the 1820's is located.

The most recent lifetime of the soul group would have been in Paris during the Surrealist Movement in Art. I have focused research on that group because so much of my efforts in this lifetime have been a continuation of helping artists as I did in that lifetime as Guillaume Apollinaire. Consequently, I have identified perhaps half of those major figures in this lifetime. These include Andre Breton, Henri Rousseau, Erik Satie, Jacques Prevert, Marcel Duhamel, Marie Laurencin, Paul Eluard, Jacques-Andre Boiffard, Alfred Jarry, Pablo Picasso and architect Le Corbusier. These are my friends in this lifetime as they were in the last, and we, somewhat, though not altogether, in jest, joke and talk about it.

A few years ago, when several of us were talking about working together on my ongoing project of staging and filming Plato's dialogues, all of a sudden, I had a stunning realization. I was talking with the same persons in this lifetime who had worked together to stage *Socrate*, a stage production based on Plato's dialogues in 1918. Not only was this during the Surrealist Period in Paris, but it was Apollinaire, who coined the phrase "Surrealist" in the program notes for *Socrate*.

That lifetime fascinates me since virtually every artist in the world knew to come to Paris at the end of the 19th Century and the beginning of the 20th Century. There were more than 15 living at one time or another in La Ruche, one old apartment building in the Montparnasse Quarter of Paris. These included Apollainaire, Marc Chagall, Nina Hamnett, Jacques Lipschitz, Amadeo Modigliani, Constantin Brancusi, Diego Rivera and others. This period of productivity was so fantastic, I've even proposed, somewhat in jest, that we begin thinking ahead, in anticipation of our next *in-between lives time* discussion, thinking about our next future lifetime. I've suggested its being in Berlin, where we could assemble at the closing of the 21st Century perhaps realizing again the wonders of the Surrealistic Period of art for a new generation. Of course, ultimately that decision would be made by the Master Spirits, but it doesn't hurt to think ahead.

Besides these vibrant friendships which are alive with ongoing research ideas and expansion of our collective consciousness—past and future, the research on the spiritual lineage continues as well. When a movie, play or book suggests yet another link or connection to the spiritual lineage that had never occurred to me, I'm off on another "chase." Nothing is more *thrilling*, than when I follow a lead—take a hint or clue and begin my research. Almost immediately I will develop a scenario of where I think it might lead. At times I have imagined it in my mind to like a chess game, visualizing Mt. Olympus, where the Master Spirits may be gathered around the table watching, waiting to see if I will make the next move they have laid out for me.

When I have developed my scenario and make the first foray into research, sometimes I am overwhelmed and exhilarated with my findings. Such was the case, for example, when I looked up the biography of Epictetus, whose writing had so captivated me as a University of Georgia undergraduate. I found that they had been recorded by Arrian. Early in my research I found that Epictetus and Arrian's relationship matched that of Socrates and Plato. In my scenario, I was trying to see how this would fit into a lineage that would have gone back and included people in my soul group, which already was including Alcibiades, Plato and Alexander the Great. If my theories were correct, I would have been in the lineage of being a companion of Alexander, and of having traveled to Sicily (Syracuse) in Plato's lifetime. I was now asking how did that author of the teachings of Epictetus fit into all of this?

When I turned the page to see what else this author of the writings of Epictetus had written, I jumped up with excitement, unable to stay in my seat. In addition to writing eight books on the teachings of Epictetus, and 12 books on his conversations (DIALOGUES!!), he had written:

1. biographies of Dion of Syracuse and two others. (Plato had gone to Syracuse at Dion's request to be tutor to the young king Dionysius II.)

2. the seven books of the *Anabasis:* the history of Alexander's march into Asia

3. the *Indike* (one book), telling about the marvels of India and the voyage home of Alexander's admiral Nearchus

4. the ten books *Events after Alexander,* known from a Byzantine summary

5. a military handbook on the best tactics in a war against the Alans—he advises to fight as Alexander had done

Arrian *remembered!* He remembered when he would have been in Syracuse as Plato with Dion and later as someone with Alexander in his march through Asia and India in a previous lifetime. His writing about them was remembering them, and, perhaps, setting the record straight. This was exactly the kind of affirmation I was looking for in my research!

Even now, I am pursuing a new realization that Arrian would have been alive, made consul of Rome, and then governor of Cappadicia, at the time Galen would have been born and started growing up in Pergamon. Pergamon would have been on the western Aegean seacoast of Asia Minor. Cappadocia would have been toward the center of Asia Minor, though one may well have had to pass near or through Pergamon to get there. Could Arrian have met and in any way influenced Galen? Arrian would have died in Athens, before Galen moved to Rome, though could they have met in Athens? Both men wrote profusely. Despite the fact that Arrian was still alive when Galen was born, I project that they are of the same spiritual lineage—being a rare case where the spirit divides. Another possibility is that of an older and younger self. In this case, a spirit would divide and a younger half would become student or friend of the older half, who would be a mentor or older teacher/friend.

Whatever the outcome of these explorations, the adventure of the continuing research goes on. It enlivens and enriches the conversations and times I have together with my friends. It continues to expand our consciousness and appreciation of life.

Remember that you have your own adventure to undertake. I used to begin my classes by saying to my students, "You are unique in all the history of the world. There has never been anyone remotely like you in all past history, nor is there anyone alive on the planet earth, nor will there ever be in future history, anyone remotely like you. You are unique in all the world." Start with the wonder and awe of that realization. A skeptical friend once asked if anyone ever found that they were a slave or servant or just an ordinary citizen in a past life. There is not such thing as "ordinary" about a human life. Each of us is a whole universe swirling about in the feeble frame of a body we call "home." There, in hidden recesses of our repressed memories, are wars, death traumas, brave deeds and heroic sacrifices waiting to be rediscovered. If we just tilled the soil under the hot sun in Assyria for one lifetime, or scaled a mountain peak in Africa in another, our present lives will be enriched by knowledge of it.

I thought of the 300 Spartan soldiers along with their King Leonidas, who sacrificed their lives fighting the Persians at the Battle of Thermopylae in 480 B.C. rather than retreat. If, for example, you were one of those soldiers in a past life, a foot soldier in that infantry, your noble and brave death is one of the greatest stories in history, greater than most rulers of countries or men of wealth recorded in the history books.

I have breakfast at a restaurant in north Atlanta on weekends, where I sit at a counter facing the food preparation area. Recently one of the workers arrived late. He strolled in fully arrayed in his hip-hop finery, with a coat thrown sort of regally over one shoulder. He walked with a kind of military, kingly arrogance. His fellow workers showed respect and admiration for an aspect of his personality or achievement, we customers would never know. I surveyed the scene and imagined him arriving home from some military battle in ancient Greece or perhaps arriving home with Napoleon's army. No matter how mundane we may feel our present lifetime is, our research could reveal a dazzling past. Start by being aware that you are living in a *messages being sent world*. Almost every thing you see or read, every experience you have is filled with meaning and contains messages. There are clues waiting to be discovered. We are living in a world with an invisible dimension where spirit guides are waiting for you to ask the questions: "Who am I?" "What is the meaning of my life?" "What is my mission in this lifetime?" They will help you find the answers.

When I was very young, there were a lot of science fiction movies about flying saucers and aliens from outer space. Usually, they would end with a melodramatic message to "watch the skies. Be alert. Listen." If we realize that we are living in a *messages being sent world,* that is not so dramatic, because messages *are* coming at us all the time. Listen for them. Hear them. Start your journey now.

APPENDIX A

SPIRITUAL LINEAGE CHARTS

While researching the spiritual lineages of those in the soul group of Yuya/Achilles/Alcibiades/Alexander/Virgil/Dante/ Lorenzo/ John Ridge/Arthur Rimbaud/Andre Breton, I was also taking notes on other spiritual lineages as well. The research techniques I used for spiritual lineage research were established initially when I did professional genealogical research over many years, prior to exploring spiritual lineages. Some of these methods in genealogy were my own methods which I developed to speed the process of establishing a family tree—starting with the oldest relatives by that name in the United States and working toward the present. At the same time I would start with the person interested in my doing research for him and working backward—starting with father, grandfather, great-grandfather, etc. This automatically gave me a wonderfully broader knowledge of the early family origins than I would have had, if I had only started back from the present time. This often cut in half the amount of time it would have taken to develop a family tree chart for the family or individual seeking my services.

In the case of researching spiritual lineages using these genealogical research techniques, applying them to "spiritual" rebirths into a new "soul group" generation, my research involved looking for specific things. These included (1) relatives, mentors or friends, who would have occupied comparable positions in relation to them in successive lifetimes, (2) similar successive personality traits—looking for the personality likes, dislikes, strengths and weaknesses to remain virtually intact in each lifetime, (3) memories of past actions, accomplishments, literary works or art which would have been repeated in a successive lifetime due to subconsciously remembering them, (4) evidences of continuing a mission from a previous lifetime, (5) unconsciously traveling or living in the places a person lived in a previous lifetime (walking on one's faded footprints without knowing it), (6) having the same profession in a following lifetime, (7) excelling in the same gifted accomplishments in successive lifetimes (like rhetoric), and other similarities which might establish a link.

I researched several lines but emphasized only two to simplify this book: The line starting with Yuya down through Andre Breton, and the line starting with Amenhotep III down through Guilliaume Apollinaire. Here are charts resulting from that research:

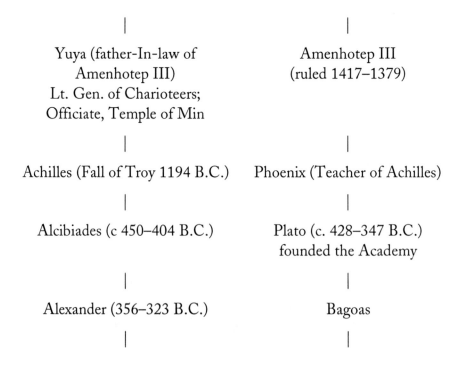

|
Yuya (father-In-law of
Amenhotep III)
Lt. Gen. of Charioteers;
Officiate, Temple of Min

|
Amenhotep III
(ruled 1417–1379)

|
Achilles (Fall of Troy 1194 B.C.)

|
Phoenix (Teacher of Achilles)

|
Alcibiades (c 450–404 B.C.)

|
Plato (c. 428–347 B.C.)
founded the Academy

|
Alexander (356–323 B.C.)

|
Bagoas

|

|

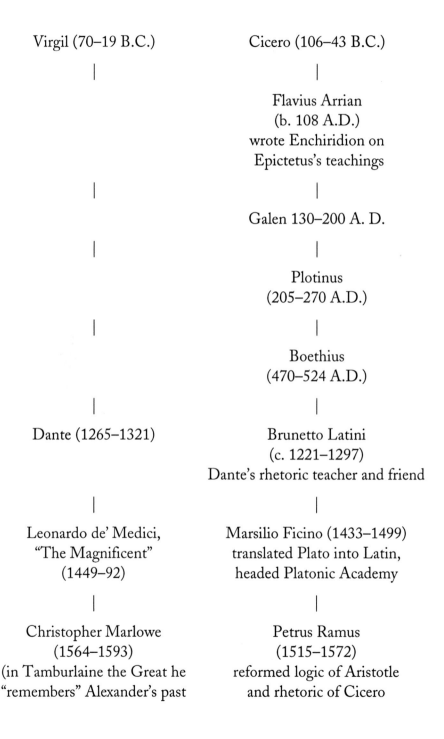

Virgil (70–19 B.C.)

Cicero (106–43 B.C.)

Flavius Arrian
(b. 108 A.D.)
wrote Enchiridion on
Epictetus's teachings

Galen 130–200 A. D.

Plotinus
(205–270 A.D.)

Boethius
(470–524 A.D.)

Dante (1265–1321)

Brunetto Latini
(c. 1221–1297)
Dante's rhetoric teacher and friend

Leonardo de' Medici,
"The Magnificent"
(1449–92)

Marsilio Ficino (1433–1499)
translated Plato into Latin,
headed Platonic Academy

Christopher Marlowe
(1564–1593)
(in Tamburlaine the Great he
"remembers" Alexander's past

Petrus Ramus
(1515–1572)
reformed logic of Aristotle
and rhetoric of Cicero

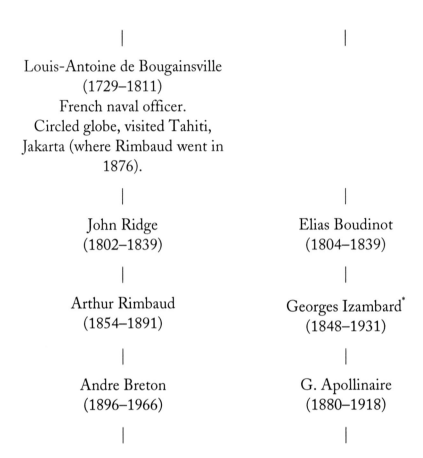

Louis-Antoine de Bougainsville
(1729–1811)
French naval officer.
Circled globe, visited Tahiti,
Jakarta (where Rimbaud went in
1876).

John Ridge
(1802–1839)

Elias Boudinot
(1804–1839)

Arthur Rimbaud
(1854–1891)

Georges Izambard*
(1848–1931)

Andre Breton
(1896–1966)

G. Apollinaire
(1880–1918)

* The flames in both the lives of Arthur Rimbaud and his teacher Georges Izambard seem to have gone out around 1874. Rimbaud's teacher and friend Izambard had his primary if not only signficance in Rimbaud's life and work before he went to Paris and met Paul Verlaine and the other Parsian poets. But by 1874 the fire in Rimbaud as well, seems to have gone out. The rest of his life Rimbaud spent wandering from place to place and making an attempt at becoming a businessman, it would appear to please his mother whose value system seemed stamped on Arthur since the age of ten. But Arthur's efforts to get rich in Africa, after he had given up on writing poetry, was a failure. His letters back home are aching with loneliness and despair. It is painful just to read them.

His early life of such profuse creativity, such explosive originality which revolutionized poetry and eventually gave birth to the Surrealist Movement, was in profound contrast to its fledgling aftermath. In addition, well after I had discovered the profound matches in time frames of the contributions and personalities of Izambard and Apollinaire, I discovered that Izambard was still alive when Apollinaire would have been born. So strong is the evidence, that the same spirit dwelt in Apollinaire that dwelt in Izambard earlier that I went in search of an explanation. That is when I discovered a tenet held by more than one New Age writer. In extreme cases, the soul may divide, and occupy two bodies at once.

In *Journey of Souls*, Michael Newton addresses this question and points out that most of his colleagues who work with past lives have listened to overlapping time chronologies—people who have lived in more than one body at times in history. Occasionally, there are three or more parallel lives. Michael Newton sees this as simply one great over-soul of energy force dividing. If it extends itself to creat our souls, then why couldn't the offspring of this intelligence have the ability to detach and them recombine, he reasons.

This leads yet to another interesting question: Since Rimbaud's creative energy seems to have left him by 20, in 1874, could his spirit have moved on to reside in another creative outburst in someone else between Rimbaud and John Ridge? It leads to yet another new concept. What if the soul group, on a new soul group mission, is assembling some other place around 1874 to move the collective message forward? Could the spirits of both Arthur Rimbaud and his mentor Georges Izambard reappeared as another student-mentor relationship somewhere else, leaving the two bodies of Rimbaud and Izambard to continue on but without the flames, which have now moved on being reborn to burn in other bodies? Whatever the explanation, I feel confident that this spiritual lineage chart is accurate and indicates the descent of these lifetimes on the chart toward the present time.

In addition to the main two lines starting with Yuya/Achilles/Alcibiades/etc. and Amenhotep III/Phoenix/Plato/etc., other lines have emerged from the research, or been suggested by it. These include:

|

Aristophanes
(450–388 B.C.)

|

Plautus
(c. 254–184 B. C.)

|

William Shakespeare
(1564–1616)
"Comedy of Errors"
is a rewrite of Plautus'
"Menaechmi" "refining
his message)

|

Pushkin
(1799–1837)
said Shakespeare
was his "master"

|

Tchaikovsky
(1840–1893)
Composed operas of
Two of Pushkin's works

|

There are two other lines, though not a part of the soul group, which appeared obvious when applying the spiritual lineageing research standards:

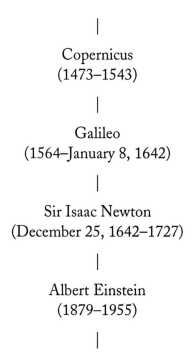

It is quite possible this line began with Aristotle (384–322 B.C.) and included Ptolemy (127–145 A.D.) Each lifetime would be an improvement on, or refinement of (continuing) the research and knowledge gained in the previous lifetime.

I have been fascinated by the phenomenon of the Harry Potter books. Especially, when I have seen interviews with J. K. Rowling, it would appear that she is "a part of something larger" than herself. After I read the first book, *Harry Potter and the Sorcerer's Stone,* I went to Europe for summer of 2000. The final part of that trip included a nostalgic return to my old college at Oxford, Regent's Park College, where I had spent a term in 1965. Pleasantly, I was assigned a room which turned out to be just two doors down from where I had stayed before.

Just opposite my door was a window, which was open slightly during the summer, so that the sound from the pub below on St. Giles welled up into my hall and into my room.

I had not bothered to pay much attention to it, until I looked through a tour guide book of Oxford, and discovered that the movie *The Shadowlands* concerned the pub, The Eagle and Child, where C. S. Lewis had met with the American woman the film was about. I decided I should visit the pub to tell my friends that I had been there.

In the pub, I asked where they had met and was directed to the little room, where they would have gotten together. Sitting there, I looked up at the wall into a picture of J. R. R. Tolkien. When I asked about his picture, then I was told about the Inklings, the group of writing friends who met there for lunch every Tuesday, and how in that little chamber *The Lord of the Rings* was read out loud for the first time to these friends as Tolkien was writing it.

Returning to the states, I realized I had never read *The Chronicles of Narnia*, but even in watching the film *The Shadowlands* again, I realized that talk of a door in a cupboard sounded very much like Harry Potter. I read the first of *The Chronicles of Narnia*, and saw other similarities. Almost instantaneously, I asked myself, "Could J. K. Rowling be a reincarnation of C. S. Lewis?" Could the Harry Potter books be an updating of *The Chronicles of Narnia*, a translating of the "message" of *The Chronicles of Narnia* to a new generation in their "updated" language?

When the fourth Harry Potter book came out, and I read that J. K. Rowling had planned seven, I went to the book store to check on the number of books there were in *The Chronicles of Narnia*. If there were seven, this would be a fit. There were seven. One might ask, couldn't someone simply consciously try to copy the idea? Of course they could. But I don't think so. What we are talking about is a subconscious activity. New Age writers might say, that in her sleep, J. K. Rowling is working with spirit guides, on the next chapters and ultimately the next books, and that may be so. I would say that, if she were C. S. Lewis in a past life, she is simply, on a subconscious level, *remembering*. Somehow, the thought that C. S. Lewis may be alive and well in the mind, life and work of J. K. Rowling provides a pleasant and comforting thought.

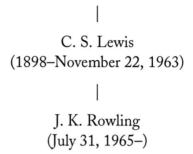

C. S. Lewis
(1898–November 22, 1963)

J. K. Rowling
(July 31, 1965–)

Among their similarities is that they both use initials in the pen names, and they both raised a child.

APPENDIX B

READINGS FOR THE THIRD MILLINEIUM

Historians believe that a mistake was made in the formulations of the Christian calendar and that Jesus was probably born in 4 B. C. Webster's Dictionary says that the beginning of the Christian Era, with what was thought to be the date of Christ's birth, was probably 4–6 B. C. The third millenium, then, began in 1996 or before.

In April, 1996, a friend, who was Head of the Horticulture Department at Berry College, recommended I read the book *Many Lives, Many Masters* by Dr. Brian Weiss. The reading of that book commenced a reading "journey," still in progress. While reading each book, I came to know what book I should read next and discovered, as I read, continuing threads of ideas logically building from one to the next.

Following is a list of the books I have read and the films I have seen, in order, as I progressed on that journey, which I have come to realize is a journey of the spirit:

Television documentary: *The Astronomers*, narrated by Richard Chamberlain (September, 1995)

Music: Enya, *Shepherd Moons* (December, 1995)

Since mid–April, 1996

Many Lives, Many Masters by Dr. Brian L. Weiss

Through Time into Healing by Dr. Brian L. Weiss

Only Love is Real by Dr. Brian L. Weiss

Life After Life by Dr. Raymond A. Moody, Jr.

Coming Back, A Psychiatrist Explores Past Life Journeys by Dr. Raymond A. Moody, Jr.

Reunions, Visionary Encounters with Departed Loved Ones by Dr. Raymond A. Moody, Jr.

The Dialogues of Plato: Phaedo on Plato's doctrine of recollection, immortality of the soul, and theory of ideas.

The Dialogues of Plato: Meno on the question can virtue be taught or learned by practice or is it the result of one's birth or nature or acquired in some other way.

The Last of the Wine by Mary Renault. A vivid historical novel about Ancient Greece, to better understand the world of Socrates and Plato.

The Sibling Society by Robert Bly

Iron John by Robert Bly (on audio tape)

The Movie: *Powder*

The Movie: *Phenomenon*

The Celestine Prophecy by James Redfield

The Tenth Insight by James Redfield

The Movie: *Philadelphia Experiment* (1984 version) referred to in *The Tenth Insight* by James Redfield

The Essential Kabbalah, The Heart of Jewish Mysticism, by Daniel C. Matt

Zohar, The Book of Splendor, Basic Readings from the Kabbalah, Edited by Gershom Scholem

The Movie: *Jesus of Montreal*

The Portable Jung, Edited by Joseph Campbell: "on synchronicity" and "The Spirit of Man, Art, and Literature—Relation of Analytical Psychology to Poetry"

The Trial of Socrates by I. F. Stone (to better understand the personalities of Socrates and Plato and democracy in Ancient Greece)

The Dialogues of Plato: *Phaedrus* on the nature and limitations of rhetoric and the nature and value of love

The Word: "Vortex"

Ishmael by Daniel Quinn

Providence by Daniel Quinn

The Hobbit by J. R. R. Tolkien

The Movie: *The Hobbit* (animation, on video)

The Play: *The Hobbit*

The Vortex/t, The Poetics of Turbulence, by Charles D. Minahen

Rimbaud, Arthur Rimbaud Complete Works, Translated by Paul Schmidt

Insights (February 28, 1997)

1. "The Astronomers" television series states that we, and everything on the planet, are composed of *star dust*, since the planet was origi-

nally a ball of fire hurled from the sun. We are walking around on a dried crust of that ball and are evolved from the energy which was a part of the forming of that crust. More accurately, then, we are cinders (defined: "any matter, as coal or wood, burned but not reduced to ashes.") Some people still possess within them "fire," others are just smoldering, while still others may seem reduced to ashes. Existential *consciousness* of our place and history within the universe keeps this fire burning. The greater the consciousness, the greater the fire. Arthur Rimbaud said that through all his veins, heavenly warmth flowed, like a fountain, like *flames* in the light of the sun.

People then could be classified as (1) flames (very intense, actively increasing in knowledge and love, and helping others—giving), (2) cinders (alert and intelligently making contributions, while being responsible), or (3) ashes (living limited, often provincial and mechanical lives, taking up space, feeding their own senses—taking).

The Story of B by Daniel Quinn

Beyond Death's Door by Maurice Rawlings

To Hell and Back by Maurice Rawlings

Journeys Out of the Body by Robert A. Monroe

Far Journeys by Robert A. Monroe

Ultimate Journey by Robert A. Monroe

Seth Speaks, The Eternal Validity of the Soul, by Jane Roberts

Soul Traveler, by Albert Taylor

Saved by the Light by Dannion Brinkley

At Peace in the Light by Dannion Brinkley

The Movie: *Wild at Heart*

The Movie: *Eden*

Leaving the Body by D. Scott Rogo

Life in Greece in Ancient Times by Paul Werner Section on the oracle at Lebadea in Boeotia entitled: "Clairvoyance in Boeotia"

Journey of Souls by Michael Newton

The Dialogues of Plato: Ion on the question "Is the artist (rhapsode in this case) a craftsman or a channel of divine inspiration?"

The Artist's Way by Julia Cameron

Way of the Peaceful Warrior by Dan Millman

The Search for a Soul: Taylor Caldwell's Psychic Lives, by Jess Stern

The Movie: *The Sixth Sense*

Harry Potter and the Sorcerer's Stone by J. K. Rowling

A Prayer for Owen Meany by John Irving

Flatland, A Romance of Many Dimensions, by Edwin A. Abbott

The Doors of Perception and *Heaven and Hell* by Aldous Huxley

Travel: Visited Oxford, England. Stayed for two weeks at college adjoining "The Eagle and Child" Pub, where the Inklings including C. S. Lewis and J. R. R. Tolkian met weekly, and where the first reading of *Lord of the Rings* took place.

The Movie: *Shadowlands* (about C. S. Lewis)

The Magician's Nephew by C. S. Lewis

Appendix C

Conclusion

Every person can begin work on his spiritual genealogy: researching his spiritual lineage.

Realize that once you focus your attention on believing that you have lived before, in other bodies in previous lifetimes, and that you can remember, then your mind is open to the possibility. This is the beginning of your effort to expand your consciousness beyond your present body and the present time.

Realize that once your thoughts "leave" your body in this quest, you will be in the realm of the Master Spirits, and you will be guided. This sounds more mystical than it is. It is simply something you will become aware of, and marvel at, when you start the process. Thoughts will be placed in your mind (like one morning, when I awoke, I had completely new insights about one of the sons of Major Ridge). A skeptic might say that it was the result of my research, and a logical connection had taken place in my mind to form a conclusion. I would say that a spirit guide was leading me in my quest for knowledge about my soul group. Often these ideas "pop into my mind" in the morning, just after I become awake. That is because, according to New Age writers, we are being coached during sleeping hours in tasks we may be facing in the new day. It is logical that being close to this condition of openness to the spiritual dimension during sleep, that we would still be receptive to this kind of information at the beginning of the day.

When you begin your quest, remember that you are in the company of a spirit guide, who will literally lead you (you may not be conscious of this) to "discover" new information. This may occur as coincidences. Conclusions may "pop into your head", which will mean they are placed there. Quite often in my search, I will take a book off the shelf, and as I lay it down on my desk, it will fall open to the page or information I am looking for. As I am working at the computer, if I have left the television set on, it will not be surprising if the actor in the movie says something that virtually fits onto the page I'm writing at the point I'm hearing it. When the movie *Finding Neverland* was on, I was writing about the soul group getting together between lifetimes and planning the future mission, when I heard the voice of one of the actors say, "To die will be an awfully big adventure." And when I was writing about the importance of fulfilling our mission in each lifetime, "Time is chasing after all of us, isn't it." And finally, when I was editing the last chapter, I heard one of the children say, "It's magical."

The most important question a person can ask is "Who am I?" We cannot know the answer to this question until we explore our many previous lifetimes, previous bodies and previous countries where we have lived to get to where we are now. One of the most important benefits of this search is that it will help you realize that you are here on a mission, and that mission connects you to your soul group of friends and family in this lifetime. We have worked together many, many times before—in different configurations. But whatever our overall mission is in this lifetime, it is a redefining or pushing forward toward improving your (our) message or mission from an earlier time.

One of the most exciting aspects of this search, is that we may have a glimpse into a future lifetime. Before I began my Reading Journey, and the conclusions resulting from it, I used to think: "How glad I am that I have lived when I did. What a mess the world is in, and I am glad I won't have to be here to clean it up." Now I realize, I will be here (in a new body), and I will have to be a part of the generation, which will have to clean it up the "mess" the present generation is making.

Where do you start, then, in your spiritual lineage research?

1. **Make a list of your favorite times in history.** This is a clue to life-times you have lived, in which dramatic or traumatic events occurred. Some of your favorite past times, hobbies, interests, fears—some of your strongest feelings may result from lifetimes lived in the periods on your list.

2. **Make a list of your favorite people in history.** This is less reliable, but it may be a clue as to a period when you have lived. For example, if King Henry VIII is one of your favorite persons in history, and you have seen every movie about him and read books about him, that is a strong clue, that you may have lived during his life-time. Anyone can be interested, of course, since he is one of the more colorful people in history, but the degree of interest here would be the clue.

3. **Make a list of your favorite period costumes.** This may be a clue.

4. **Make a list of all the places you have lived.** Think of them in terms of places you may have lived before. There is a strong possibility that you have lived within a hundred mile radius of where you are living now in some previous lifetime.

5. **Analyze any passion you have that seems to be extreme.** If someone says you are a "nut" about something, this may be a clue concerning something you have done before. This would explain your passion, and it would be consistent on following up on a project or mission started in a previous lifetime.

6. **Make a list of everyone you may consider to be in your present soul group.** According to Michael Newton in *Journey of Souls*, the smaller sub-group primary clusters vary in number. It could contain

anywhere from three to twenty-five souls. The average in a soul group is around fifteen. This is called the inner circle.

The smaller circle in the soul group will remain close throughout all eternity. Usually this consists, quite logically of family members and/or closest friends. This may seem logical in this lifetime, something we've never questioned, but remember that in past lives, you would have the same personalities but in a different configuration. You son or daughter in this lifetime could have been your parent or sibling in a past lifetime. I have heard of sons who act like fathers to their fathers, or daughters acting like mothers to their mothers. In a past lifetime, they may have been, and simply carried over that relationship in this lifetime.

The larger number of your soul group may continue to become apparent to you throughout your life. You may know someone when they are young, and they move away. Then, almost mysteriously, they may move back and live just down the street, and be in your church or temple, and you may find yourself on a committee with them. In my case I found that I have often been a "mentor" and friend. My father in this lifetime, turned out to be an uncle in a previous lifetime, but was an extremely strong personality. With him, in a previous lifetime, I worked closely as though he were a father in that lifetime.

7. **Analyze your profession, your father's profession, the kind of work your closest friends do.** Are there any similarities of interests or volunteer work, or passions that stand out? Your friends and/or business or professional associates may not only meet at work, but in a volunteer capacity which you both care more about than the work on your job?

8. **Especially observe if one of these groups of contemporary workers or friends, have the same interests in places, persons in history, places in history, hobbies, etc.** This similarity may be a clue that you were together in that place or doing that thing (before) in an

ongoing soul group. If you have a mentor, teacher, minister or older friend, who seems more like a father (or mother) to you than your own, remember they may have been in a past lifetime. Once these pieces of the puzzle are laid out on a table, exactly like the old jigsaw puzzles of my youth, then we begin the process of fitting the pieces together to see what fits.

It may start with one striking unexplainable incident, like my reaction to seeing the film about Arthur Rimbaud. From that you begin to build as I did. It may be an unexplainable passion for a place, like I had for the Daffodil Farm, or someone (whom you may have been married to in a previous lifetime, or a sibling or parent in a previous lifetime) who is a close friend in this lifetime. Remember, it is *your* adventure. Perhaps the main thing is, it will make us aware of how limited, but important our lifetimes of the present really are, and how significant they become when we see that our personalities result from a long succession of dramatic and meaningful lifetimes in many wonderful and exotic places.

The main thing to remember in your research is that this effort will expand your knowledge and consciousness of who you are in the universe and why you are here. It will give you a sense of direction and purpose. It will make you more conscious of your family and friends and their importance in your life.

Most important, I hope, it will make you aware that you are surrounded by loving spirits (possibly those of your parents, relatives or friends whom you knew earlier and who are already in the spirit world, and Master Spirits like Athena helping Telemachus in *The Odyssey*).

These Master Spirits are ready to aid you in this quest. Even in something as simple as plain genealogy, I remember one of the librarians in the library in Rome, Georgia, telling me about a woman from Alabama, who could not find a missing link in her research for past ancestors. The librarian told me that the woman had a dream, and in the dream, she was told to go to the Rome, Georgia library, and there she would find what she was looking for. The next day, she got up, drove to Rome, came to the library and found exactly what she had been looking for. The librarian said, "That is not the first time something like that has happened. It happens all the time."

So, realize that you will have help in this quest, not unlike these genealogists, who were aided in being "told" to come to the Rome Library.

In trying to understand your spiritual origins, and the journey and life of your spirit down through eternity, why shouldn't you expect at least this kind of assistance? And remember, your aid will come from the world of the Spirit, and in that world nothing is impossible.

Remember, there will be skeptics who will say, "None of this can be proven." To those who want to reject the mysterious in life, and boil everything down to the two dimensional question of whether or not it can be proven, let me add that the concept of "proof" itself is a myth and an illusion. It is a human illusion of certainty.

When I was in high school I was taught that there are 92 elements in chemistry, and there were—at that time. By 2006 there were 109 named elements. We are told certain quantitative facts about our solar system and universe, but this information is changing with each new discovery, and the certainty of our "absolute" knowledge comes apart.

When I began studying genealogy, I thought the most infallible historical "facts" were in the Federal Census figures, such as those starting with 1850 and recorded every ten years. Then I discovered that over a period of 30 years or three census records, we could have a person's name spelled three different ways, and his age given as three different ages. Some historians write a history book with a bone to pick (with entirely subjective motivations), or for the ego satisfaction of getting the publicity. Some are not qualified to do historical research, and their work is filled with errors. (I have run into several in these last categories.) This may lead to a second myth, and that is the truth or infallibility of the printed word. Errors can easily be made in print by faulty research—quoting a previous historian, who is quoting someone else whose research is inaccurate—or simply by a poor typist, who makes mistakes.

The important thing about attempting to learn about the lineage of our eternal spirits—of remembering from our past lives—is that that learning experience will expand our knowledge of ourselves and our universe. It will place us in a better position to make this a better world.

Bibliography

Abbott, Edwin Abbott. *Flatland: A Romance of Many Dimensions*. Princeton, New Jersey, Princeton University Press, 1991.

Apollinaire, Guillaume. *Apollinaire on Art: Essays and Reviews 1902–1918*, edited by LeRoy C. Breunig Boston, MFA Publications, A Division of the Museum of Fine Arts, Boston, 2001.

Bly, Robert. *Iron John: A Book About Men*. New York, Vintage Books, A Division of Random House, Inc., 1992.

Bly, Robert. *The Sibling Society*. New York, Vintage Books, A Division of Random House, Inc., 1996.

Brandon, Ruth. *Surreal Lives: The Surrealists 1917–1945*. New York, Grove Press, 1999.

Brinkley, Dannion; with Paul Perry, introduction by Raymond A. Moody, Jr. *Saved by the Light*. New York, Harper Paperbacks, A Division of HarperCollinsPublishers, 1995.

Brinkley, Dannion; with Paul Perry; foreword by James Redfield. *At Peace in the Light*. New York, HarperTorch, An Imprint of HarperCollinsPublishers, 2002.

Cameron, Julia. *The Artist's Way: A Spiritual Path to Higher Creativity*. New York, Jeremy P. Tarcher/Putnam a member of Penguin Putnam, Inc., 1996.

Carpenter, Humphrey. *The Inklings:* C. S. Lewis, J. R. R. Tolkien, *Charles Williams and their friends.* London, HarperCollinsPublishers, 1997.

Carpenter, Humphrey. *J. R. R. Tolkien: A Biography.* New York, Houghton Mifflin Company, 2000.

Dante. *The Divine Comedy: Volume I Inferno.* Translated by Musa, Mark. New York, Penguin Books, 1984.

Ehle, John. *Trail of Tears: The Rise and Fall of the Cherokee Nation.* Anchor Books, A Division of Random House, Inc., 1989.

Everitt, Anthony. *Cicero: The Life and Times of Rome's Greatest Politician.* New York, Random House Trade Paperbacks, 2003.

Franck, Dan. *Bohemian Paris: Picasso, Modigliani, Matisse, and the birth of Modern Art.* New York, Grove Press, 2001.

Gill, Anton. *Art Lover: A Biography of Peggy Guggenheim.* New York, Perennial, An Imprint of HarperCollinsPublishers, 2002.

Hibbert, Christopher. *The House of the Medici: Its Rise and Fall.* New York, Morrow Quill Paperbacks, 1980.

Hollander, Robert. *Dante: A Life in Works.* New Haven, Connecticut, Yale University Press, 2001.

Homer, *The Odyssey.* Translated by W. H. D. Rouse. New York, Mentor, and imprint of Dutton Signet, a division of Penguin Books, 1937.

Homer, *The Iliad.* Translated by Robert Fitzgerald, Introduction by Andrew Ford. New York, Farrar, Straus and Giroux, 2004.

Irving, John. *A Prayer for Owen Meany.* New York, Ballantine Books. 1997.

Jung, Carl. *The Portable Jung: Edited by Joseph Campbell*. New York, Penguin Books, 1976.

Lewis, C. S. *The Chronicles of Narnia: The Magician's Nephew*. New York, Harper Trophy, A Division of HarperCollinsPublishers, 1994.

Mailer, Norman. *Picasso as a Young Man: An Interpretive Biography*. New York, Warner Books, A Time Warner Company, 1996.

Matt, Daniel C. *The Essential Kabbalah: The Heart of Jewish Mysticism*. New York, HarperSanFrancisco, An Imprint of HarperCollins-Publishers, Inc., 1995.

Millman, Dan. *Way of the Peaceful Warrior: A Book that Changes Lives*. Tiburon, California, H J Kramer, Inc., 1984.

Minahen, Charles D. *Vortex/t: the Poetics of Turbulence*. University Park Pennsylvania, The Pennsylvania State University Press, 1992.

Monroe, Robert A. *Journeys Out of Body*. New York, Main Street Books, Doubleday, 1977.

Monroe, Robert A. *Far Journeys*. New York, Main Street Books, Doubleday, 1985.

Monroe, Robert A. *Ultimate Journey*. New York, Main Street Books, Doubleday, 1994.

Moody, Jr., Raymond A. *Life After Life*. New York, Bantam Books, 1988.

Moody, Jr., Raymond A., with Paul Perry. *Coming Back: A Psychiatrist Explores Past Life Journeys*. New York, Bantam Books, 1992.

Moody, Jr., Raymond A. with Paul Perry. *Reunions: Visionary Encounters with Departed Loved Ones*. New York, Ivy Books, Published by Ballantine Books, 1993.

Newton, Michael. *Journey of Souls: Case Studies of Life Between Lives*. St. Paul, Minnesota, Llewellyn Publications, 1998

O'Brien, John Maxwell. *Alexander the Great: The Invisible Enemy*. London and New York, Routledge, 1994.

Plato. *Plato Complete Works*. Edited by John M. Cooper. Associate Editor D. S. Hutchinson. Indianapolis/Cambridge, Hackett Publishing Company, 1997.

Plato. *Early Socratic Dialogues*. Edited with a general introduction by Trevor J. Saunders. New York, Penguin Books, 1987.

Plato. *The Dialogues of Plato*. Introduction by Erich Segal. New York, A Bantam Book, 1986.

Plato. *The Republic and Other Works*. Translated by B. Jowett. New York, An Anchor Book, Published by Doubleday, 1989.

Plutarch. *Plutarch: The Lives of the Noble Grecians and Romans*. Vol. II. The Dryden translation, edited and revised by Clough, Arthur Hugh. New York, The Modern Library, 1992.

Quinn, Daniel. *Ishmael*. New York, A Bantam/Turner Book, 1995.

Quinn, Daniel. *Providence: The Story of a Fifty-Year Vision Quest*. New York, Bantam Books, 1996.

Quinn, Daniel. *The Story of B*. New York, A Bantam Book, 1996.

Rawlings, Maurice. *Beyond Death's Door*. New York, Bantam Books, 1979.

Rawlings, Maurice. *To Hell and Back*. Nashville, The Charioteer. Thomas Nelson Publishers, 1993.

Redfield, James. *The Celestine Prophecy*. New York, Warner Books, A Time Warner Company, 1993.

Redfield, James. *The Tenth Insight: Holding the Vision*. New York, Warner Books. A Time Warner Company, 1996.

Redford, Donald B. *Akhenaten: The Heretic King*. Princeton, New Jersey, Princeton University Press, 1984.

Renault, Mary. *Fire from Heaven*. New York, Popular Library Eagle Books, 1969.

Renault, Mary. *The Charioteer*. New York, A Bantam Book, 1974.

Renault, Mary. *The Mask of Apollo*. New York, Bantam Books, 1966.

Renault, Mary. *The Persian Boy*. New York, Pantheon Books, a division of Random House, 1972.

Renault, Mary. *The Praise Singer*. New York, Pantheon Books, a division of Random House, 1978.

Renault, Mary. *The Last of the Wine*. New York, Vintage Books, A Division of Random House, Inc., 2001

Richardson, John. *A Life of Picasso: The Early Years, Volume I 1881–1906*. New York, Random House, 1991.

Richardson, John. *A Life of Picasso: Volume II: 1907–1917*. New York, Random House, 1996.

Rimbaud, Arthur. Schmidt, Paul, Translator. *Arthur Rimbaud Complete Works*. New York, Harper & Row Publishers, 1975.

Robb, Graham. *Rimbaud.* New York, W. W. Norton & Company, 2001.

Roberts, Jane. *Seth Speaks: The Eternal Validity of the Soul.* Including Notes by Robert F. Butts. San Rafael, CA, Amber-Allen Publishing, 1994.

Rogo, D. Scott. *Leaving the Body: A Complete Guide to Astral Projection.* New York, A Fireside Book, Published by Simon & Schuster, 1983.

Rowling, J. K. *Harry Potter and the Sorcerer's Stone.* New York, Scholastic, Inc., 1998.

Rowling, J. K. *Harry Potter and the Chamber of Secrets.* New York, Scholastic, Inc., 1999.

Rowling, J. K. *Harry Potter and the Prisoner of Azkaban.* New York, Scholastic, Inc., 1999.

Rowling, J. K. *Harry Potter and the Goblet of Fire.* New York, Scholastic, Inc., 2000.

Rowling, J. K. *Harry Potter and the Order of the Phoenix.* New York, Arthur A. Levine Books, An Imprint of Scholastic Press, 2003.

Scholem, Gershom. *Zohar: The Book of Splendor.* New York, Schocken Books, 1995.

Stack, Rick. *Out-of-Body Adventures: 30 Days to the Most Exciting Experience in Your Life.* Chicago, Contemporary Books, An Imprint of NTC/Contemporary Publishing Company, 1988.

Shattuick, Roger. *The Banquet Years: The origins of the avant-garde in France 1885 to World War I—Alfred Jarry, Henri Rousseau, Erik Satie, Guillaume Apollinaire.* New York, Vintage Books, A Division of Random House, 1968.

Sommers, Christina Hoff Sommers. *The War Against Boys: How Misguided Feminism is Harming our Young Men*, New York, Simon & Schuster, 2000.

Starkie, Enid. *Arthur Rimbaud.* New York, A New Directions Book, New Directions Publishing Corp., 1968.

Stone, I. F., *The Trial of Socrates.* New York, Anchor Books, Doubleday. 1989.

Taylor, Albert. *Soul Traveler.* New York, A Dutton Book, Published by the Penguin Group, 1998.

Tiger, Lionel. *The Decline of Males*, New York, St. Martin's Griffin, 2000.

Tolkien, J. R. R. *The Hobbit.* New York, Ballantine Books, 1982.

Vergil. *The Aeneid.* A New Translation by Patric Dickinson. New York, Mentor, Penguin Books, 1961.

Waldberg, Patrick. *Surrealism.* New York, Thames and Hudson, Inc., 1997.

Watkins, Susan M. *Conversations with Seth: The Story of Jane Roberts's ESP Class.* Portsmouth, New Hampshire, Moment Point Press, 1999.

Weiss, Brian. *Many Lives, Many Masters.* New York, A Fireside Book, Published by Simon & Schuster, Inc., 1988.

Weiss, Brian. *Through Time Into Healing.* New York, Simon & Schuster, Inc., 1992.

Weiss, Brian. *Only Love is Real.* New York, Warner Books, Inc., 1996.

Wilkins, Thurman. *Cherokee Tragedy: The Ridge Family and the Decimation of a People*. Norman Oklahoma, University of Oklahoma Press, 1986.

Wolf, Fred Alan. *Parallel Universes: The Search for Other Worlds*. New York, A Touchstone Book, Published by Simon & Schuster, 1990.

About the Author

William E. Bray received the Master of Education degree from Johns Hopkins University and the Master of Divinity degree from Yale. His undergraduate degree is from the University of Georgia where he majored in history and philosophy. He studied psychology at Oxford and completed Harvard's Institute of Arts Administration. After serving in ministerial positions in Connecticut, Maryland and Georgia, he served as an assistant professor of psychology at the University of Baltimore and Endicott College and as an instructor in psychology and the humanities at Georgia Highlands College. At the University of Baltimore, he established the film department and founded the Baltimore Experimental Film Society. He was director of community arts organizations in Delaware and Georgia and was President of the Georgia Assembly of Community Arts Agencies. He was founder of the Georgia Fine Arts Academy where he was director for 20 years. He is author of *The Emasculation of Men in America: 50 Reasons Why Males are No Longer Men* and *Your Spiritual Lineage: Researching the Genealogy of Your Soul.* William Bray lives in Atlanta, across the street from where Margaret Mitchell spent the last three years writing her epic novel *Gone With the Wind* and a block from the childhood home of author James Dickey.

978-0-595-39516-3
0-595-39516-3

Printed in the United States
108375LV00004B/258/A